First Printing: 2023
ISBN 978-1-954158-24-5
Layout by Marty Dundics
Cover and interior illustrations by Xeth Feinberg
Edited by Brian Boone

Humorist Books is an imprint of *Weekly Humorist* owned and operated by Humorist Media LLC.

Weekly Humorist is a weekly humor publication, subscribe online at weeklyhumorist.com

110 Wall Street New York, NY 10005

weeklyhumorist.com - humoristbooks.com - humoristmedia.com

HUMORIST BOOKS

New York

For Michael Gerber and his amazing American Bystander

What Am I Doing Here?

A "Simpsons" Writer Visits the World's Hellholes So You Don't Have To

Written by Mike Reiss
Photos by Denise Reiss

Contents

Contents

Chapter 1

WELCOME TO MY WORLD

"You Wanted to Come Here..."

My wife and I had just spent a week in Pakistan's Kelasha Valleys, attending their annual pagan ceremony. They called it a Moon Festival, but it was really just seven days of goat beheadings, a non-stop French Revolution for goats. It was… interesting, but I was eager to get the hell out of there. That's when we learned that the only road out of the valley had been destroyed by a landslide the night before. The one bulldozer in the region had been brought in to clear the road, but it got stuck in the mud and slipped off its treads. It was now dangling halfway off a mountain path, threatening to crush the village far below. The bulldozer that was supposed to rescue us had now made the problem much, much worse. Our only way out was to crawl over it.

As we dragged our luggage over the mud-caked bulldozer treads, dangling two hundred feet above the valley floor, I said to my wife, "You wanted to come here."

It's a line I've used a lot over the years – when we were abducted in Honduras; when we were interrogated in Iran; when we were robbed in Rio on the day we arrived – twice.

In thirty-four years of marriage, my wife has dragged me like a battered valise to one hundred and forty-five countries and both Poles. Lately, we've been hitting the -stans: Paki-, Kazakh-, and Uzbeki-. She's now looking into a trip Afghani-, for reasons I don't quite under-. Whatever. To quote an old Choctaw proverb, "Happy wife, happy life."

Denise is an indefatigable and intrepid traveler. I, on the other hand, am easily fatiguable and highly trepid. Perhaps it's our age difference: I'm sixty-one while she's a sprightly fifty-eleven.

More likely this problem, like every problem in every marriage, can be blamed on our childhoods. As a girl, Denise and her mother traveled around the world three times. They went to places I never heard of (like Peshawar) and places I'd heard of but thought were imaginary (like the Kingdom of Swat). They were not rich people, but these were the days of "Europe on $5 a Day" and "India on a Nickel a Month." Denise and her mom loved traveling and her Dad loved having the house to himself.

In my home, travel was something to be dreaded. Every summer, my dad would jam his five screaming kids into a station wagon and drive us to Civil War sites. Every summer another battlefield. Our family photo album could have been shot by Matthew Brady.

I met Denise in 1977, when she was studying at Harvard and I was at Harvard not studying. She was, and is, brilliant, buoyant, and ridiculously beautiful. Denise is frequently mistaken for Nicole Kidman, while I look like a bag of wet garbage.

I married up, she settled, and we both know it.

I love my wife and she loves to travel, so I go wherever she tells me. This is not an uncommon situation. Women think men are insensitive brutes – and we is– but there are so many things we do to please them that we would never do on our own. These include: attending Broadway shows; going to any non-sports museum; shopping for anything other than food and underwear; watching "Dancing with the Stars," "So You Think You Can Dance," or "Now That's What I Call Dancing"; buying homes, having children, and wearing pants. As Abraham Lincoln said in his Second Inaugural Address, "Happy wife, happy life."

Denise and I got married in late 1988, just before the Berlin Wall fell. The Germans got their freedom, I lost mine, and so far it's working out all around. Throughout our courtship, I'd been putting in hundred-hour weeks, writing TV shows like "The Simpsons," "It's Garry Shandling's Show" and "ALF." The honeymoon would be the first trip we ever took together. We'd each narrowed our list of destinations to two: I suggested Disneyland or Disneyworld; Denise pitched Yemen or Siberia.

"Uh, honey," I told her gently, "those are places people want to get out of."

In the end, we compromised. I chose Hawaii and Denise picked the very worst part of it: Kauai. Kauai is a lovely place to have a horrible vacation. That's why they filmed "Jurassic Park" there. Or at least, they tried to, until a typhoon hit.

Our honeymoon was five days of non-stop rain. We took an all-day sightseeing bus tour, but the only sight to see was thick, blanketing fog.

"I'm sorry about this," I told Denise. "You can't predict these things."

"Sure you can," she said. "Kauai is the rainiest spot on earth!"

(Denise waits to drop these bombshells on me until the end of a trip. As we were leaving Papua, New Guinea after a week's visit, she thought to mention, "Oh, by the way, they eat people here.")

That Denise chose the wettest place on earth for our honeymoon tells you two things about her:

1. My Wife Fears the Sun

She's not afraid to visit a war zone or an oppressive dictatorship, but a sunny day scares the living crap out of her. Before she leaves the house, she bundles up like a beekeeper: long sleeves, long pants gloves, scarf, and broad-brimmed hat. I've seen women in burqas tell her to loosen up. But all this protection has served her well. Even in our sixties, Denise has the skin of an adolescent while I have the skin of an avocado.

Denise will book us a trip to some tropical paradise, and then spend the days holed up in dark museums. We only hit the beaches after sunset, like snorkeling vampires. In fact she may be a vampire. She doesn't age. She hates garlic. And she sleeps in a coffin.

I'm just kidding. She loves garlic.

2. My Wife Likes Extreme Destinations

After visiting the wettest place on earth, Denise took me to the driest place on earth (the Atacama Desert), the highest (Mount Everest), the lowest (the Dead Sea), and the dullest (her twenty-fifth high school reunion).

I regard every new trip the way I regard every new US President: a little hope, a lot of fear, and the belief that somehow I will survive this.

It's like Polonius told Hamlet, "Happy wife, happy life."

Bienvenido
BIKINI BEACH

Denise dresses for Bikini Beach.

Why Travel?

"Why travel?" my Grampa Abie used to say. "Anywhere you go, there's a Broadway and a Main Street." These were strange words coming from him, who had an excellent reason to travel from Poland – Hitler! My grandfather came to America alone, a young boy with just eight cents in his pocket. By the end of his life, he had doubled that.

Grampa did have a point: Much of the world is exactly the same. But that's one of the most exciting surprises of travel: the strange, exotic places you fear are just like home. Santiago, Chile, is exactly like Los Angeles: home to a thriving film industry, and choked with traffic, pollution, and overpriced restaurants. Tehran, Iran, is even more like LA, so much so that thousands of Iranians have resettled there. They call it Tehrangeles.

Here's a short list of places that are like other places:

KIEV:	Chicago
IRAQ:	Arizona
BANGKOK:	Las Vegas without gambling
DUBAI:	Bangkok without booze
HELSINKI:	Muncie, Indiana
HONDURAS:	Hell

Despite the similarities, there are tiny differences that make every country fascinating:
- In Hong Kong, air conditioning is set to meat-locker coldness.
- In Peru, corn on the cob is the size of a football.
- Chile is so long and skinny, it doesn't fit on maps. They have to cut it in half and put the two parts side by side.
- Luggage carts are free in airports in every country but ours
- In Costa Rica they call speed bumps "dead policemen"!
- In Asia, they don't say "1, 2, 3" when they're taking a picture. They say "3, 2, 1." I know, crazy, right?

Of course, the main reason you travel is because the world is full of things you have to go there to see – they won't come to you. Being there is different than a virtual experience. To put it in terms my Probable Reader will understand, it's like the difference between sex and porn. Travel is like sex: It's expensive, time-consuming, and often to be regretted. It can be messy and require a trip to the doctor. I can only do it two, three times a year. But then I can brag to all my friends about it.

Travel delivers! The world's landmarks have been drawing visitors for centuries; if the Grand Canyon were overrated, news would have reached Yelp! by now.

The Great Pyramids really are great.

The Great Wall of China is great, too.

But "The Great Waldo Pepper" is a lousy movie. (Although it stars Robert Redford, and he's great. And older than the Pyramids.)

Machu Picchu, high in the Andes, is cloaked in mystery and magic… until you actually visit. Then you'll recognize it instantly for what it is: a summer resort. A place in the mountains for noble families to escape the heat of Peru. It's got cabins, it's got views. There's even a slide for the kiddies. Really. It's just an old Catskills resort, but for the Incas, not the Finkels.

Naturally, travel comes with disappointments. The Mona Lisa is much smaller than you expect – about the size of a sheet of typing paper. But The Last Supper is friggin' huge.

Oscar Wilde called Niagara Falls "the second great disappointment in a bride's life." While this was almost certainly true for Mrs. Wilde, Mrs. Reiss and I love Niagara Falls. It's beautiful and overpowering and breath-taking… for about an hour. And when you get bored with it, you can walk up the road to Clifton Hill, home to every delightfully crappy attraction you could hope for:
- Dinosaur Mini-Golf
- Harry Potter Rip-off Indoor Putt-Putt Golf
- Zombie Laser Tag
- The Movieland Wax Museum, The Criminals' Wax Museum, The Sports Heroes Wax Museum (O.J. was in all three!)

Get on the Bus

For our first anniversary, Denise wanted to go to Iraq but I hadn't even been to Ireland. Clearly I needed to play some catch-up, so we embarked on a survey tour – a cheap bus trip that roared across Europe faster than the German army. It was a grueling trip, but we were young back then. The other forty-two people on the trip ranged in age from really old to "why aren't you dead?"

Our tour guide, the man who would be our constant companion and lifeline for the next two weeks, came onboard. Even from the back of the bus I could tell this guy was an alcoholic and was jonesing for a drink badly. "I am Frasier Johnson and I do not wish to be here," he announced in a British headmaster voice. "I was supposed to be on Christmas holiday with Mother, but your scheduled tour director became unavailable. There is a toilet in the back of the bus. Don't use it. I do not intend to drive your poo across Europe for the next two weeks."

I turned to my wife. "You wanted to come—"

"Shaddup," she replied. The honeymoon was over.

The itinerary somehow brought us to eighteen countries in fourteen days. A typical day: Wake up before sunrise in Milan, three hours on the bus to Pisa, ten minutes at the Leaning Tower, back on the bus for a four-hour drive to Rome, arriving after dark when nothing's open. One passenger called it "A Tour of the CLOSED Signs of Europe."

The hotels they parked us in were cheap and way out of town. And breakfast every morning, in every country, was Cocoa Puffs. Somehow, Europe got the memo that Americans love these little poison pellets of "chocolate." It's a cereal so bad, even its cartoon bird mascot has gone insane.

The thing that struck me most was how profoundly dumb our fellow passengers seemed. There was an old man from Virginia whose wife called him Superman, for some reason. He had no understanding of foreign currency and was constantly being swindled by souvenir sellers. Interpol seemed to be steering European con men towards him.

One morning he came in to Cocoa Puffs wearing a Tyrolean hat with a fake feather in it.

SUPERMAN: Lookee this hat. Only cost me five bucks American.

ME (EXAMINING PRICE TAG): Actually, you paid fifty bucks.

SUPERMAN: Dang!

Another day, we were being led through the basement of the Vatican en route to the Sistine Chapel. As we passed through the Pope's boiler room, Superman leaned over to me and asked, "Did we see it yet?"

I was amazed a man could survive to old age being this stupid. And I was distressed to learn he had passed his genes on to ten children and thirty-eight grandchildren. I guess that's why his wife called him Superman.

Then there was the guy who somehow managed to find an Irish pub in every country we visited. When I asked him how his evening went, he always had one of two replies:

"It was great. They played 'Danny Boy' and 'When Irish Eyes Are Smiling.'"

Or:

"It was terrible. They didn't play 'Danny Boy' or 'When Irish Eyes Are Smiling.'"

This man seemed to judge all human existence by this single criterion. I thought he was a simpleton, so I asked him what he did for a living.

"I'm the Deputy Director of the Centers for Disease Control."

He wasn't a dope. He just liked what he liked.

Then there was Fred Frumkin from Fort Myers, Florida. (I didn't make that up. I wouldn't. I couldn't.) He'd always ask the strangest, most niggling questions of every tour guide:

- Do all guillotine blades slant in the same direction?
- Were there models for the Notre Dame gargoyles?
- Did chamber pots freeze up on winter nights? How would you clean them?

I'd never seen a mind that worked like his.

"I write instruction manuals for a living," he explained.

Another member of the group was an electrician from the Bronx. No matter how awe-inspiring the cathedral or castle we visited, this guy couldn't take his eyes off the wiring. When we toured Windsor Castle, he pointed to an overloaded outlet with cords snaking under a medieval carpet.

"See that? Someday this place is gonna go up like a Roman candle."

Two years later it did.

I grew to really like this group. Except for Superman, they weren't dumb at all. They may not have been worldly or sophisticated, but they were out there trying. They weren't old farts, sitting home in their rockers. They were off their rockers.

I enjoyed the trip and I made a lot of good friends, none of whom I ever saw or spoke to again.

As I left the bus, I handed a nice tip to our irascible guide Frasier. He stared at the cash in his hand, baffled. In four decades as a prickly tour guide, he'd never been tipped before.

A lot of funny stories came out of that trip, enough to fill a great comedy movie. Or, in my case, a godawful comedy movie. I wrote a screenplay about a tour group in Greece called "My Life in Ruins." The critics liked the cleverness of the title and nothing else. The movie got a nine percent on Rotten Tomatoes, putting it five percent below "Howard the Duck" and eleven points below "Cats." "Cats"!

The worst review came from my father. I invited my parents to the premiere and when the movie ended he turned to my mother and said, "You wanted to come here?"

SIDE TRIP: The Worst Tour Guides on Earth!

Our tour guide on the European bus tour was a short-tempered, misanthropic alcoholic. But I've had worse.

Take Dave Fellner, who took a group through South America. He was disorganized, wasting hours on paperwork when we should have been touring. He kept us baking in a hot bus for an hour while he read us his terrible poetry. But mostly, I hated Dave's bad toupee. It was a red mop that perched askew on his head, fooling no one. It looked like something grave robbers stole from the tomb of Harpo Marx. And he insisted on balancing a goofy sun hat on top of the wig. Why? The toupee was already a hat. He wore a hat on a hat. Dave brought us down the Amazon – Brazilian tribesmen, who'd never seen a white man before, spotted this thing. "Bad rug," they hooted. "Shatner."

We were sailing down another river, the Nile, in a felucca – a wooden boat propelled by a single, triangular sail. We drifted noiselessly under a fat Egyptian moon: just me, the wife, the boat pilot, and our tour guide Afshan. I don't speak Arabic, but I could tell Afshan had gently asked the pilot to stop looking at his phone. He gently told her to go felucca herself. At this point, Afshan lost it. She started screaming at the pilot as we made our way down the Nile. She was loud, angry, and like a trained opera star, never had to pause for breath. Her screams were non-stop, echoing off the ancient temples on either side.

When the ride ended, Afshan hustled us off the boat, still yelling about the pilot. She took us to the National Museum, but instead of showing us around, she just kept screaming. Finally, she threw us in a cab, screamed us goodnight, and sent us on our way.

The next day she came to our hotel to apologize. She'd been under a lot of stress, her mother was in the hospital, and then she had to put up WITH THAT GODDAM BOAT PILOT. She was off and screaming again. I'd heard the phrase "to lose one's shit," but I'd never seen it in person before. This woman had literally lost her shit. I pictured her tacking up posters reading "LOST: MY SHIT. HAVE YOU SEEN IT?"

We had another tour guide in Egypt named Rusty. This either referred to his red hair or his rusty brain beneath it. Rusty gave long rambling lectures on Egyptology, even though he knew little English and fewer details: "Cleopatra was around. The pyramids was around. Lots of dead people was around. (LONG PAUSE) Sand was around."

Rusty is part of a large subset of travel professionals: the tour guide who is no help whatsoever. They come in two categories, like shrimp: sweet and sour.

Here's an exchange I had with a sweet guide in France:

ME: How long has this church been here?

GUIDE #1: Eighty-five feet, monsieur.

ME: No, how long? When was it built?

GUIDE #1: Yes, it was built.

ME: Okay, so it's not a natural rock formation.

GUIDE #1: No. Lunch is included, but no soft drinks.

ME: Well, that's an excellent answer to a question I did not ask.

GUIDE #1: The bathroom is down the hall to the left-right. Just go upstairs to the basement.

At least this guy was nice. My guide in Ghana was spoiling for a fight.

ME: Was this a prison?

GUIDE #2: No!

ME: The sign says it was a prison.

GUIDE #2: No, it's a place where they keep bad mans.

ME: A prison.

GUIDE #2: No, it's, how you call it, where you put prisoners.

ME: A jail? A brig? A dungeon? A hoosegow?

GUIDE #2: No! It is a prison!

ME: Ohhhh…

These two guides lived five thousand miles apart. It's too bad they'd never meet. They'd have made a great comedy team.

Chapter 2

OUR WEIRD, WEIRD, WORLD

've decided to start this book with a bang – my motto is hook 'em early, disappoint 'em later. As such, I'm opening with a whirlwind tour of four continents, taking you to the weirdest countries on earth. They are rarely visited by tourists and seem to operate by their own rules.

Of course, you don't have to read book this straight through. Feel free to skip around. Then stop skipping around – you look like a fool. Sit down and read the goddam book. But enjoy these stories in any order you please. Like Tolstoy, I write my books to be read on the toilet.

Would that be funnier with Pushkin?

Bolivia Wild!

Our story begins two miles above sea level and ends deep in the bowels of the earth, drinking shots with Satan. We are visiting Bolivia, hands down the strangest country on earth.

Like many lunatics, Bolivia has a very normal face it shows the public. The entire eastern half of the country is lush and jungle-y, boasting Spanish-style towns with charming plazas. The only weirdness here is that they have a capital city called Sucre that isn't really the capital. And that the Spanish Inquisition didn't end here until 1834.

This is the sensible place to start a trip to Bolivia. You spend a few days in the warm, low-altitude region, working your way slowly west to the chilly heights of the Andes. Of course, we didn't do that. We took an overnight flight straight to La Paz. At ten thousand feet, it's the highest capital city in the world. We were sleep-deprived and low on oxygen and began hallucinating almost immediately. I seemed to be greeted by dozens of tiny indigenous women, dressed in native serapes… and English bowler hats. It looked like a nationwide meeting of the Sons of the Desert, the Laurel & Hardy Fan Club.

And then I realized I WASN'T hallucinating. All the native women were wearing brown English derbies. It seems in the 1920s a shipment of bowler hats was ordered for workers building the Bolivian railway. The hats they got were too small, so they were peddled to the local women. They've been wearing them ever since, making La Paz look like a casting call for an all-Mayan production of "Waiting for Godot."

And that's appropriate, because Bolivia is totally surreal. The deserts sprout forests made of stone – they're giant rock crystals that look just like trees. Beneath them are bubbling hot springs that are cold to the touch – natural gas seeps through frigid water making it look like it's at full boil.

Then there's the two lakes, one a frightening blood-red, the other an inviting emerald green. But the scary lake is teeming with wildlife, feeding off its red algae. And the green one is eerily deserted, because its color comes from arsenic in the water.

And what do you think Bolivia's most popular music is? Salsa? Samba? Rhumba? Mambo? Try classical German Baroque. German missionaries brought the music to Bolivia in the eighteenth century, and like the bowler hats, it stuck. If you're wondering where the next Johann Sebastian Bach is coming from, it might be the jungles of the Amazon.

But the weird thing that brought us to Bolivia, is four thousand square miles of nothing – a veritable Connecticut of nothing. Some would say Connecticut is a Connecticut of nothing, but screw you. I grew up there. We have Mark Twain's house and… a couple of big casinos. That's about it.

The nothing I'm referring to is the Great Bolivian Salt Flat. It's just hard, white salt stretching flat and featureless in every direction. It's a Salvador Dali landscape or, if you've taken Art History, a DiChirico landscape.

Nothing prepares you for this much nothing. I drank a Coke then looked for somewhere to set the can down – but there wasn't a bump or a rise for forty miles. After the Coke, I had to pee, but there wasn't a tree to block me or a rock to crouch behind. I walked a thousand yards away and was still in plain view of my guide and my wife. There was nowhere to hide.

There were more surprises down the road – well, if there were roads. Everyone drives straight across the plain, Mad Maxing it. Every few hundred miles you'd spot a hotel, rising from the dust like a mirage. And they're all beautiful: gorgeous and stylish and comfy and unique. They didn't have to be. The weary traveler would have settled for anything: a Motel 6. A Motel 3, even.

We headed deep into the heart of Bolivia, the scenery changing constantly and randomly: mountain, desert, jungle, mountain, jungle, and then for about ten miles, Mars. It looked just like Mars. And just beyond that you hit Amish Country. A large community of Amish have settled in central Bolivia because why not? It's a totally random country, the Mad Libs of nations.

We finally reached our destination: the graves of Butch Cassidy and the Sundance Kid. If you remember the film, or, you know, actual history, Butch and Sundance fled America for Bolivia, where they were gunned down by the Bolivian army. They were laid to rest in a tiny cemetery, unremembered and unvisited. It's in a small town in the middle of nowhere – actually a mining camp where a hundred families lived in company housing. We'd heard the town had a Butch and Sundance Museum, so we had the sheriff open it up – this is the same guy who unlocked the cemetery for us. Being sheriff meant he had all the keys.

It was a nifty museum once you brushed aside the decades of dust: It was unremembered and unvisited, too. The locals who'd spent their lives in this town had no idea the museum was there. At least two dozen of them came with us to see it for the first time. There were possessions from Butch and Sundance, props from the movie, and, yes, more bowler hats.

But now we come to the weirdest encounter in this weird trip to this weird country. We went to the mountain of Potosi, in the town of Potosi in the municipality of Potosi. It's as close to a mountain of pure silver as you'll find anywhere outside a fairy tale. At one point, sixty percent of earth's silver production came out of Potosi. It made Bolivia rich and independent – it's

the reason Bolivia's its own country and not just some salty part of Peru. Need proof? Bolivia put a picture of the mountain, front and center, on their flag.

Silver has been pulled out of the mountain for five hundred years, and there's plenty left. That's why there are still independent miners working in Potosi, digging in all directions, like a human ant farm. It's dangerous work – over the centuries, eight hundred thousand miners have died inside the mountain. My wife was trying to make it eight hundred thousand and two. She persuaded a mine operator to let us inside. But this was no tour – this place would get a "holy fuck!" on Tripadvisor. The tunnels were dark, narrow, and crumbling. All around us were miners setting off dynamite. There was no plan, no map. We just crawled and slithered our way down toward the heart of the mountain. At one point I squeezed my entire body through a tiny crack and plopped into an enormous open space. It was like being born, but even more traumatic.

I found myself in a large, empty chamber. Then, I turned… and seated behind me was: Satan.

Satan!

SATAN!

It was an eight-foot tall sculpture of Satan, seated on a throne. It was crude, roughly carved, and painted, but it made an impact: It had large, red, pointy ears, and a larger, redder, pointier erection. Yes, Satan had a boner. He was surrounded by packs of cigarettes and mini-bottles of liquor, gifts from indigenous miners. Every morning they'd share a shot of grain alcohol with Satan, asking him to keep them safe during the work ahead. At the end of the day, they'd do more shots with Satan, as a way of saying, "Thanks for not killing me."

And because I had no idea how to get out of there, I did the same. I drank an airline bottle of booze with Satan and asked for his help. I did a second shot and told him to get my wife out, too. And we did make it back to the surface, bruised, scraped, and filthy.

What can I say? Prayer works.

Bhutan is guided by a simple philosophy: "Gross National Happiness." It's one of those great tourist slogans like "Virginia is for lovers" (it's not) or "Molokai is for Lepers" (it was…). "Gross National Happiness" is one of the most compelling three-word phrases since "love thy neighbor" or "Where's the beef?"

I'd always assumed some ad agency came up with it over endless cans of Coke and late-night lines of coke. But no, the phrase just spilled from the lips of the Fourth King of Bhutan, during a 1972 interview. And it does suit this tiny sliver of a country, wedged between China and India. Our driver explained, "We are stuck between two superpowers, each with a billion people and nuclear weapons. We have to be nice to everybody." Our driver, by the way, was also physician to the Royal Family. And a past candidate for President of Bhutan. It's a small country. And a delightfully odd one.

They do everything a little differently. Their national costume for men is a plaid bathrobe, black ankle socks, and loafers. Everyone looks like a '60s Dad who ran out on his lawn at three a.m. to check for burglars.

Their national dish is melted cheese with spicy hot pepper. It's nachos, but without the chips. It's also the world's first smoke-free country. Seriously – if you want a cigarette, you have to step outside to Bangladesh to smoke it.

The Bhutanese even have their own way of bathing. You lie naked in what is basically a horse trough full of water. Then they add hot rocks at one end of the tub to heat it. Want a warmer bath? Add more rocks. Want it colder? Too bad – it only gets hotter. It's very low-tech and extremely soothing.

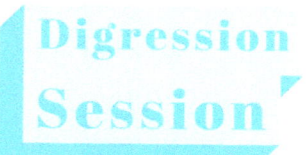

Digression Session

And now a digression on baths around the world.

One of the great adventures in traveling is to try the local bath. In Turkey, I had a Turkish bath: You go from a hot sauna to a cold pool to a warm bath and repeat. Then you get rubbed down with warm oil, which they scrape off with a dull razor. It was very relaxing, except when I'd look across the room and see two burly Turks rubbing down my naked wife. When it's over, you actually feel both brand new, but also like a part of history – this is the exact kind of bath that the ancient Romans took; the same one my Jewish ancestors took in the Turkish baths of Brooklyn. How can you not love an experience shared by Julius Caesar and Sid Caesar?

And counting New York's gay baths, Cesar Romero. Yes, I just outed Cesar Romero.

I never felt cleaner than after my Turkish bath; and I never felt dirtier than splashing around in a Colombian mud volcano. It was warm and gooey fun. This is the rare bath where you are filthier coming out than going in. It's a bath you need a bath after.

And at the Pilsner Urquell Brewery in the Czech Republic, I took a beer bath. I sat in a wooden tub soaking in unfermented ale, with hops and barley floating around me. I asked the tour guide if there was some health benefit to all this. He said, "Nah. It's just something for tourists."

Bhutan truly has achieved Gross National Happiness. The people are always smiling. And so are the dogs.

As Mahatma Gandhi said, "The greatness of a nation and its moral progress can be judged by the way its animals are treated." And the dogs of Bhutan are treated very well: No one owns them, they just roam from house to house, knowing they'll get food and a warm place to sleep. They're fat and happy and they do something I've never seen other dogs do: smile. They sit on the edge of the road, stare out at the vast Himalayan landscape, and grin. Life is good.

It's truly a fairy tale kingdom, and it's ruled by a real-life Prince Charming. They call him King Jimmy – he's an Oxford graduate and an international heartthrob. He's drop-dead gorgeous, and he married a beautiful commoner, a real-life Cinderella.

The most famous buildings in the country, the ones you see on all the travel posters, are a complex of monasteries called the Tiger's Nest. It was built in 1692, half a mile straight up, right into the mountains. As one poet put it: The buildings cling to the mountain like a gecko. Poets love gassing about the place: They named a ravine "The Copper Colored Mountain of Paradise"; they called a plateau "The Path of a Hundred Thousand Fairies." Really? A hundred thousand? I counted maybe eighty thousand fairies, tops.

Whatever they call it, it's a brutal three-hour hike to get to the Tiger's Nest and it's all the tourists talk about:

"Did you do it? I didn't do it. I don't know if I can do it. Should I do it? You do it and tell me if I can do it."

Folks, you can do it. It's like the seventeenth century monks said, "Let's build something that chubby Americans can get to – but just barely. Let's ruin their vacation." I did it and I'm sixty years old and largely made of dough. It was a tough climb but worth it for the awe-inspiring temples, the breath-taking views, and that smug sense of pointless accomplishment.

You can do it. I did it so you can do it. So just do it. Did you do it yet? I did.

I loved everything about Bhutan except its main eco tourist attraction: the black-necked crane. Our driver kept talking about it, and we were intrigued because we thought he was saying "the buck-naked crane." Every year, countless cranes migrate from southern Tibet to a remote Bhutan valley.

Well, they say they're countless, but you can count them -- there's only about two hundred of them. And their "migration" is only sixty-six miles – in Los Angeles, that's called a commute. And the government keeps visitors a mile away from them. They're invisible to the naked eye. But through powerful binoculars they look like table salt spilled on a pool table.

There's a six-mile path around their nesting place but it's a bullshit hike. I mean that literally – it's grazing land for cattle so you are walking through six miles of bullshit.

What was I doing here?

I came to Bhutan to see my friend Eames Demetrios.

And now a digression on Eames Demetrios.

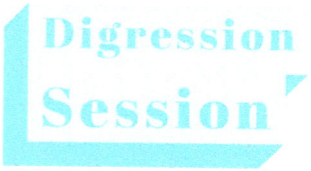

Jesus, another digression? All right. Eames Demetrios is the grandson of famed designer Charles Eames. His other grandfather is a sculptor and his father is a sculptor, too. Most impressive to me, his grandmother wrote and illustrated the kid's book "Mike Mulligan and His Steam Shovel." Eames is an artist too – what choice did he have? If he'd become a heart surgeon it would bring shame to the family.

Eames works in conceptual art. He travels the world installing historical monuments to events that never happened. They have an otherworldly look and recount a detailed history of the Kcymaerxthaere, a race of people that I'm pretty sure he made up. Eames has a secret dream: "Someday, after a nuclear holocaust, future archeologists will find my monuments and take them to be the true history of life on Earth."

We traveled with Eames across Bhutan, looking for the perfect spot to erect one of his phony-baloney monuments. And he found it: a rock outcrop jutting from a hill on a Bhutanese farm. He marched into the tumble-down farmhouse on a mission: to explain to these peasant farmers what conceptual art was, what his project was, and why they should let a perfect stranger build something weird on their property. Oh, and he didn't speak Bhutanese and they didn't speak English.

Five minutes later, he emerged from the farmhouse: "Done and done."

He actually got this thing built. You can see pictures if you Google "Kcymaerxthaere Bhutan." That's KCYMAERXTHAERE: k-c-y-m-a... you're not gonna Google it.

This is all cool stuff but none of it explains why I consider Bhutan one of the weirdest spots on earth. This country makes the list because of ALL ITS PENISES. There are giant throbbing erections everywhere you look. They're painted all over people's homes, in candy-colored pinks and yellows. They're three, four, five feet long, and there's nothing stylized about them – these dongs have veins. They've got balls. It makes you wonder: How do you vandalize a house that already has penises painted all over it? Don't believe me? Google it. This I bet you will Google.

There are dongs hanging from the rooftops, painted on street signs – there are whole gift shops selling nothing but souvenir wieners.

It all reminds me of a great joke from the 1950s: A playboy has lured a co-ed back to his bachelor pad. She picks up a sculpture and asks: "What is this?"

He says, "It's a phallic symbol."

She says, "Wow. I don't wanna tell you what it looks like."

The man behind Bhutan's obsession with dangling dingles is their spiritual leader Drupka Kunley. He was a fifteenth century monk who fired an arrow from Tibet, vowing to preach wherever it landed… and it came to rest in Bhutan. He was a literal Saint, but he was no saint. He drank, he philandered, he told dirty jokes, and he preached boozy sermons. They called him The Divine Madman – he was the perfect combination of Gautama Buddha and Gary Busey.

How can you not love a country that picks that for their religious leader?

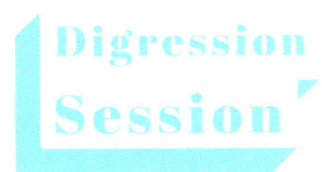

And now a final digression on fact-checking.

Full disclosure: This chapter includes well-known quotes from the Fourth King of Bhutan and Mahatma Gandhi. You can find both all over the Internet. But in-depth research reveals that both quotes are bogus – they never said 'em. And that Tiger's Nest monastery? Yes, it was built in 1692, but it burned down, so the one you actually see was constructed in 1998. Also, Tigers don't build Nests. And Drukpa Kunley couldn't possibly have shot an arrow from Tibet to Bhutan – that's two hundred miles. Even if it landed there, how would he have found it?

I've learned my lesson. In the future, I will no longer do in-depth research.

That's *The* Sudan to You

We boarded a bus in southern Egypt. It was filled with people carrying things you would never think to bring on a bus: dishwashers, refrigerators, a hundred-pound bag of onions, a piano. The bus rolled exactly five feet, when everyone – people, appliances, onions – was ordered off. That was the whole ride. After a quick three hours in customs, we entered The Sudan.

By the way, it's THE Sudan. The '"The" is part of the name, like The Bronx, or The Situation from "Jersey Shore." It sounds classy, but the name just translates to "The Black People" to distinguish them from The Beige People of Egypt.

The title of this book could not be more apropos than in the case of The Sudan. About halfway through our visit, I asked my wife, "What are we doing here?"

"I don't know," she said. To this day, we can't figure out why we went. It's like we'd been drugged and woken up naked on the streets of Khartoum. In two weeks there, we never saw another tourist. In every hotel we stayed in, we were the only guests. Mind you, their hotels aren't exactly hotels – they're just large, pleasant buildings with dozens of cots scattered around. No lobby, no café, no staff. It had the feeling of a large college dormitory just after a bomb scare.

Similarly, The Sudan's restaurants aren't restaurants – they're just open kitchens, with tables and chairs, scattered along the side of the road. You bring your own food, you cook it yourself, you bus your own table… and then you buy a Coke from the owner, so he can pretend he's running a restaurant.

Self-deception is common in The Sudan. Although no one visits, the locals think it's crawling with tourists. "It's never been so busy," said our tour guide, gesturing to an absolutely empty expanse of desert. "It's getting too crowded." The Sudan is a nation of Miss Havishams, expecting a wedding to break out at any minute.

We stumbled on one honest-to-goodness luxury resort in the country. It was Christmas Day, what would have been the height of tourist season if they had one, and the resort was completely deserted. I'm sure of this because every door to every room in the place was wide open, proclaiming its existential emptiness. I thought this might be a nice Christmas gift to my wife, so I inquired about booking a room.

"Eight hundred dollars a night," the manager told me. Perhaps his price point was the reason he had no guests. It was a nice place, but the going rate for a hotel room in the Sudan was fifteen bucks a night.

"Could you go any lower?" I asked.

"No," he replied. "We are completely full."

No room at the inn. On Christmas. In the desert. Jesus.

The Sudan's main claim to fame, and an excellent reason to visit, is that they have more pyramids than Egypt. They're not as big as the Great Pyramids, but there are plenty that are thirty, forty, fifty feet tall. And they are lousy with them: The Sudan has pyramids like Seattle has coffee shops. As a result, the Sudanese are not particularly protective of their cultural heritage: You can climb these pyramids, you can camp in front of them, if you could fit one on your lap, I'm sure they'd let you take it on the bus. They're pretty easygoing people.

I learned this when we were trying to drive across the Nile, and the ferry broke down. Or, to be more specific, the donkey who pulled the rope that towed the ferry had broken down and gone to sleep. We were stuck, and so was the truck driver behind us. But instead of cursing and pointlessly honking his horn, this driver stripped naked, grabbed a bar of soap, and jumped in the Nile for a bath. Then, so did my tour guide. And then, so did I. I sank a foot deep into the rich Nile mud – this was the silt that flooded Egypt every year, turning a desert into fertile farmland. This is the mud that made civilization.

"I like it!" I said. The words just came out of me.

"I like it!" repeated the truck driver. "I like it!" He didn't speak English, but he enjoyed the sound of it.

After we crossed the Nile, we ran into the truck driver at a stoplight. He leaned out his window and said, "I like it!"

Then we ran into him in a different city two days later, and he said it again: "I like it!" For all I know, he's still saying it. Non-stop. Like a loon.

I'd gotten to love crazy Sudan. I found it hard to leave – literally. We were driving through a small village when a farmer waved us into his home. We were the first, and quite possibly the last, tourists he had ever seen. As our host poured us endless cups of tea and Coke, I noticed that this humble farmer's house was ginormous – maybe ten thousand square feet of rooms and enclosed courtyards. This was typical of the region – cinder blocks were cheap, and land was even cheaper, so why shouldn't four people live in a fifty-room house?

When we left the farmer's home, his neighbors invited us into their McMansion. And then his neighbor's neighbors, and his neighbor's neighbor's neighbors. I could have done this forever, endlessly abusing the nation's hospitality, but all the tea and Cokes were giving me caffeine psychosis. It was time to leave The Sudan.

Sudanese airports are so confusing, so mismanaged, so corrupt, that our tour guide hired a professional to cut through all the red tape: The Enforcer. He was a huge man, six-foot-six, apparently constructed of cinder blocks himself. With his shaved head, he looked like the convict from The Green Mile, except his magical power was the ability to navigate Khartoum Airport. He got us there six hours early, and then we stood back and watched as this African Colossus moved from one line to another, filling out forms, intimidating, wheedling, and possibly bribing officials.

By the time The Enforcer got back to us with our boarding passes, he appeared to have shrunk noticeably. Khartoum Airport had broken him. There were actually tears in his eyes.

"They just make it so hard," he sobbed.

"There, there, Gigantor," I said, patting his massive back. "There there."

I still have no idea why I went to The Sudan. But… "I like it!"

My writing partner and I had an idea for a sitcom called "Twenty Below." It was about a team of scientists living together at the South Pole. It was a cross between "The Big Bang Theory" and "Frozen" before either of those things were things. Of course, no network would buy it. The first executive we brought it to said, "Instead of the South Pole make it the North Pole."

"We can't," I said.

"What's the difference?"

"It's literally all the difference in the world," I said. "The South Pole is on land – that's why you can build a base there. There are no stations at the North Pole – it's just a mass of floating ice."

"I still think it should be the North Pole."

I asked him why.

"It's a funnier Pole."

Well, my wife has dragged me on trips to the North Pole and the South Pole. She even found a third pole for us to visit, in her never-ending quest to make sure I die broke. In this chapter, we'll visit all three poles – and you can decide which one is funniest.

We booked a cruise to Antarctica; it left out of Ushuaia, Argentina, the southernmost city on earth. After checking in onboard, my wife wanted to explore the town. It speaks volumes for Ushuaia that one of their top tourist attractions is a prison. Another one is a large sign that says Ushuaia.

We returned to our ship to find the entire crew furious – they had to delay the start of the cruise for four hours while waiting for us. During the next week, the number one topic at dinner was, "I wonder who those idiots were that held up our launch."

Although I never got busted for this, fate caught up to me in another way. One evening, for shipboard entertainment, they had "Tell a Joke Night." Passengers got up and told their favorite joke – the jokes were all sexist, racist, or filthy, and they all got huge laughs. I decided to elevate the evening with some of my own comedy. I've lectured in five hundred venues in twenty-two countries and have lots of stories that have never failed.

Well, they failed that night. I kept going and going, hoping to get a pity laugh, so I could leave the stage gracefully. After ten minutes, I gave up. It's bad to bomb, but it's worse to bomb on a cruise ship, because you're stuck with the audience that hated you. For the next seven days, everyone on the boat avoided me. The only other entertainment onboard was a magician. Unfortunately for him, he performed on a stage that had mirrors on the back, on the sides, and on the ceiling. This allowed you to see how he did every single trick. Next cruise I take, I'm doing his act.

On a quick tangent, I had a very different problem on another cruise. There was a very funny ship's comedian named Noodles Levenstein – that's his actual pasta – and he looked just like me. For the rest of the cruise I was pestered by fans thinking I was Noodles.

PASSENGER #1: "You were very funny last night."

ME: "Yes I was. How do you know?"

PASSENGER #2: "Is that your real name?"

ME: "Mike? Yes it is."

Noodles, I lost you a lot of fans.

Since this is a book of me whining about my bad vacations, I don't have much to say about Antarctica. It's a glorious cruise – I've done it twice, and I recommend it to all of you. You visit during their summer, so the sun

shines twenty-four hours a day. The scenery is always changing – you see lots of icebergs, none of which look like that pointy guy that sank the Titanic. Icebergs are round, they're square, some have archways that look like enormous mouseholes, and many, I swear, look like floating office buildings. And they're not all white - they come in pastel colors - blue, pink, and green. You also see whales – so many whales you won't get off your deck chair to see them unless they're traveling with a baby – or making one. I like to watch whale sex.

Which reminds me of a joke.

A little boy and his mother are whale-watching. The boy points to the orca's eight-foot erection and asks, "What's that?"

The mother says, "That's, uh, nothing."

Later, the boy is whale-watching with his father and he points to the orca's penis. "I showed that to Mom and she said it's nothing."

And his father says, "I spoiled her."

ANYWAY… Antarctica is surprisingly warm too – under all that ice is the largest desert on earth. Summer temperatures are generally in the forties and one day it hit fifty. I saw penguins lying prostrate on the beach, schvitzing from the heat. And if you like penguins, you'll see tens of thousands of them. They're packed onto every exposed rock in the ocean. I learned two things from the animated film "Happy Feet": One is "don't see "Happy Feet Two.'" The other is that not all penguins are alike: There are many different species, each with their own personality: Chinstrap penguins are nasty punks, gentoos are easygoing schmucks, and macaroni penguins are ugly little bastards.

My one disappointment: There's no pole at the South Pole, no red-and-white striped post with a big knob on top. Cartoons had steered me wrong. If I wanted to see the real pole, in all its candy cane glory, I guess I'd have to head to the Arctic.

A trip to the North Pole is nothing like going to the south. The only way to cruise there is on a Russian icebreaker. It's not luxurious, but the constant sound of cracking ice is actually soothing: It's like taking your car down a gravel driveway eight hundred miles long. It's so relaxing, nobody minded that there was nothing to do. The ship had no phone, no internet, no TV, not even "Tell a Joke Night." I'd expected the teens onboard to go full "Lord of the Flies," but they were fine with it. The only entertainment the Russian crew offered was a tour of the ship's nuclear reactor. They even allowed me to touch it, which I did but probably shouldn't have. Now I can't have children.

Once again, there was tolerable weather and all-day sunshine, but not a lot to see. Just an unbroken expanse of flat white ice. You'd spot the occasional polar bear, a fair amount of polar bear poop, and then more ice. This was a trip with a very arbitrary destination, an imaginary geographical point. Just over a hundred ships had made this voyage in all of human history. This cruise was for the jaded traveler, the person who'd been everywhere else. A hot topic at dinner was "which is better: the east coast of Greenland or west coast?" The passengers consisted of large Chinese and Indian families. It was a good indicator of where the money is today, because this was an expensive cruise. How expensive? I have no idea. My wife just kept telling me : "You can afford this." That's not much help. I can afford an elephant too, but I don't want to buy one.

We finally reached the geographic pole, and it looked like all the other ice we'd been seeing for a week. Still, the crew tried to make it special: They set up a barbecue. The purser dressed as a mermaid. They inflated a hot air balloon – it took us a hundred feet up, to get a panoramic view of the miles and miles of nothin'. A guide brought us on a hike – he carried a rifle, in case we encountered a polar bear. Not that he would have used it: If you kill a polar bear in the Arctic you are literally tried as a murderer. If a polar bear showed up, the guide would be better off shooting us.

The crew erected a British-style phone booth where you were allowed to make one call: We phoned my mother-in-law, not realizing it was three in the morning where she was. The call scared her half to death. Good times.

As a finale, they cut a hole in the ice, so anyone who wanted could take an icy plunge in the Arctic Ocean. I wondered, "Who is stupid enough to do this?" Answer: every single person on the ship except me. Even an eighty-year-old lady did it. When she came out, the Russians gave her a shot of vodka, which, medically speaking, is the worst possible thing you can do.

My wife goes swimming at the North Pole.

The crew did a great job of making something out of nothing. But I was still disappointed: There was no pole at the pole. I'm not crazy to think this. At one point, metal workers actually made two candy cane striped poles. One went on a tour of America, appearing in parades as The Real North Pole. The other one was dumped out of the back of a cargo plane somewhere over the Arctic. This was the fifties – people did stuff like that.

When we made it to the North Pole, I told my wife, "Well, I've done it – I've followed you to the ends of the earth." It was my way of saying, "No more travel, okay?" Not okay. Denise found another North Pole and dragged me off to it.

NERD: "Technically speaking, there are several North Poles. The geographic pole, the magnetic pole, the geo-magnetic pole—"

ME: "Shut up, nerd! Shut up shut up shut up!"

NERD: "Stop. You're scaring me!"

We took a trip to the town of North Pole, Alaska, a suburb on the outskirts of Fairbanks. North Pole got its name the way most things get their names in Alaska – in 1944, someone who lived there called the place North Pole, and everyone else said, "Sure. What the hell." It's now got year-round Christmas decorations and streets named Santa Claus Lane, Kris Kringle Drive, St. Nicholas Drive, and a swamp called the Thirty Mile Slough.

We did all the fun things you can do in North Pole, Alaska: ice fishing, dog sled racing, snow mobiling, more ice fishing, more dog sled racing. Four days is a long time to kill there. They may sound exciting, but these are all activities that can be done by a corpse. On a dog sled, you're just ballast. In ice fishing, you're just a pole holder. Snow mobiling involves steering so you don't hit a tree – otherwise there's nothing to it. It's like driving in a very loud, very rickety Miata, in freezing weather with the top down. Plus, in Alaska, they call snowmobiles snow machines. Why? Someone once called them that, and everyone else said, "Sure. What the hell."

The lack of activity in their activities may explain something about the Alaskans: Although they lead robust, outdoorsy lives, sixty-seven percent of them are overweight. And though they love their independence and isolation, the ones I met had clearly been alone too long: They're loud and chatty, they laugh at their own jokes, and they strike up long conversations with anyone who's passing by. Nice folks.

The main reason we visited this North Pole was to see the Northern Lights. We caught a glimpse of them the first night and they were just wispy gray clouds – like the fireworks you see on the Fifth of July. (Not the Fourth – the Fifth! Ya get it?) The next two nights we spent hours in subzero weather looking for them, but it was too cloudy. Our final night, we hired a professional: a full-time aurora chaser. He was a former cop, driving a van equipped with radar and state-of-the-art cameras. He drove us all over central Alaska, looking for a break in the clouds. By midnight, I was ready to quit, but he was just getting started. He parked on top of a mountain and waited, muttering to himself: "C'mon, Lady Aurora. I know you're out there. Show yourself." The other five tourists in the van nodded off. We were all hostage to this man's obsession. And that's when it hit me: He was a policeman. This was a stake-out. And the Northern Lights were his perp.

Finally, at four a.m. – FOUR A.M.! – he threw in the towel. Like a depressing '70s cop movie, justice had failed. Aurora never showed her pretty face. Dames.

But, on our way out of town, headed for the airport, we saw something even better: the North Pole pole! Remember that metal pole they made for parades across America? Somebody found it, rusting and forgotten in a junkyard, and set it up on a suburban street corner. I'd gone from one end of the globe to the other looking for it, and here it was, on the one road without a cute name in North Pole, Alaska. My quest was over.

Was it worth all the trouble, all the expense, all those hours in freezing cold? You better believe it wasn't. It wasn't at all.

SIDE TRIP: Mike's Fake Mailbag

nd now a letter from Mike's Fake Mailbag, where we answer questions from fans we couldn't possibly have yet.

Dear Mike,

I'm only two chapters into your book and I'm wondering... Aren't you scared you'll die on one of these trips?

Sincerely,
Sue Donymous
Bad Pun, MI

Thanks for your fake letter, Sue. The answer is no, I'm not scared that I might die on one of these trips. I am absolutely certain I will die on one of these trips. The only question is how.

- We were on Pakistani Air's flight from LA to Lahore when a flight attendant handed me the local paper. The cover story from the previous day? "Pakistani Air Flight from LA to Lahore Crashes with No Survivors."
- Ethiopia is a gorgeous country with an exceptionally mild climate. That's because all its villages are built on high plateaus, accessible only by steep crumbling dirt roads. Every day, in every village, I could look out the window of my tour bus and see another tour bus lying wrecked, upside down, at the bottom of a ravine.
- We went to the Winter Olympics in Pyeongchang, South Korea. This was a huge event and this small, onion-growing town was not quite up to the challenge. We attended the Opening Ceremony, sitting in the frigid outdoor arena for four hours. It ended at midnight, and seventy thousand attendees poured into the parking lot to find... one bus. We waited in the freezing cold as the bus ferried people away, fifty at a time. Around three a.m., it was our turn to ride the bus. (Actually, it wasn't – we brazenly cut the line. We were freezing and New Yorkers.) The bus drove for twenty minutes, and dumped us in the middle of nowhere, ten miles outside of town. They had no plan. They were just leaving the tourists there to die.

We took a trip to The Sudan, which up until recently had been a war zone. And while we were there, a bomb went off – in a Dumpster outside our New York home. So you see, you're not really safe anywhere.

We survived all this, and we survived that snake in the toilet in Uganda. But somehow, somewhere, I will die on one of these trips. And my life will flash before my eyes, all hundred and forty countries we visited parading past me. My death will be just like the It's a Small World ride. Now that scares me.

In Ghana, I pester a live alligator because my guide told me to.

Chapter 3

WHAT AM I DOING IN EUROPE?

don't need to tell you about Europe. You've probably been there, and it's exactly what you expected. The French are rude. The Swiss are polite. The Austrians are polite in a way that feels rude: They can say "thank you" and make it feel like "up yours."

But some things make more sense when you're actually there. Denise and I stayed in a hotel on the edge of Germany's Black Forest, the setting for so many Grimm fairy tales. We stepped into the woods for a little stroll and immediately became as lost as Hansel and Gretel. We wandered helpless and hopeless for over three hours before we finally were rescued by a brave woodsman. (Actually, it was the gardener from the hotel – we were only fifty feet from the property.)

Still, there are a few corners of the continent you never thought of visiting. Let me take you there…

Charming Chernobyl

I made a trip to a little country called Ukraine. Maybe you've heard of it.

It's the largest country in Europe, rich in farmland, flat as a blini, with no mountains or canyons to protect it. This makes it an absolutely perfect place to invade, and people have been doing just that for centuries: the Russians, the Poles, Austro-Hungary, the Turks, the Russians again, and finally Rudy Giuliani. As I write this, they're besieged by Russia yet again. Ukraine is like that sweet, harmless kid that everyone in school just loved to pick on. In other words, me.

Once, Ukraine even invaded itself. In Kiev, there's a Russian tank mounted on a pedestal as a World War II memorial. In 2014, Pro-Russian separatists drove the tank off the pedestal and used it to take over a local arts center. At least some of the blame goes to Ukraine for leaving the keys in the tank.

And there's that other Ukrainian oopsie, Chernobyl.

In 1985, a meltdown at this nuclear power plant killed thirty and forced hundreds of thousands to flee. Now it's a tourist attraction, albeit one that exposes you to plutonium, cesium, strontium, and, yes, americium. (USA! USA!) It sounds dangerous, but tour operators do issue some protective gear: little paper booties. These are not to safeguard you – you already paid admission – but to protect the linoleum floors of the reactor. The one sop to safety is that every guest is given a badge to detect radiation. At the end of the tour, you turn in the badge; three weeks later you'll get a call if you've received a lethal dose of radiation and have three weeks to live. I'm not making any of this up including this part: They now have nighttime tours of Haunted Chernobyl, in case nuclear apocalypse wasn't scary enough. Oh, they also host bridal showers.

My wife, who loves dangerous, stupid adventures (such as marrying me) could not wait to visit Chernobyl. And so, back in 2011, she booked us a romantic two-week trip to Ukraine. (By the way, it's just Ukraine, not "The Ukraine." It's like U2's Bono, not U2's "The Edge.") Our trip began in southern Ukraine, in the picturesque seaside town of Odessa. Like most Eastern European beaches, there's no sand – just a waterfront stretch of gravel. And no one actually goes in the water – they lay in beach chairs all day, without sunscreen, burning and blistering audibly. Walking by, it sounded and smelled like bacon frying.

This is where I first noticed something unique about Ukraine, something you never read in the papers: Everyone in the country has big boobs. Maybe it's genetics, maybe it's diet, maybe it's a side-effect of Chernobyl. Regardless of the cause (who cares, eh lads?), everyone in this country is stacked: young women, old women, and many of the men. And nobody's hiding it: there are low-cut blouses, tight T-shirts, and tank tops everywhere you turn. This is the country I dreamed of when I was sixteen (and sixty!). It was the Sovereign Republic of Cleavage. It was the nation of Boobistan. It was Knockerslovakia.

Odessa boasts a world-class opera house, where, for just three dollars, I attended the greatest performance of "Aida" I ever slept through. But the city's main attraction is the Odessa Steps, an elegant flight of stairs leading from the city to the harbor. It was here that Sergei Eisenstein filmed the "Odessa Steps massacre" sequence for his 1925 silent classic "The Battleship Potemkin." This brutally beautiful montage was ripped off by Brian DePalma for the best scene in "The Untouchables," and has been parodied in dozens of comedies, most of them by Woody Allen. On a more somber note, it was on this very spot in 1905 that nothing happened. Eisenstein made up the whole massacre. Pure Bolshoi! Fake newsreel!

From Odessa, we drove through two hundred miles of solid nothing to reach Pobuzke, home to the Museum of Strategic Rocket Forces. It's situated in the middle of a giant wheat field, littered with disarmed nuclear missiles the size of school buses. (At least I think they're disarmed – they did leave the keys in that tank.) Hidden in the center of the field is an elevator that takes you one hundred feet down into a missile silo. The doors open on what looks like Adam West's Batcave: a large underground command center filled with blinking consoles, rotary phones, and 1960s-era computers. Every morning for years, a Russian soldier strapped himself into a chair and waited for the phone call that gave him the order to push the button to launch the missile that would incinerate New York City. Decades later, that same Russian soldier was still down here, working as a tour guide. I'm not sure anyone told him the Cold War was over.

Ironically, the nuclear missile silo was not the scariest place we visited in Pobuzke – our hotel was. I first sensed trouble when our driver dumped us at the front door and sped off, like a frightened coachman bringing guests to Dracula's Castle. It was the only hotel in town, and it was run by an Ogress. She was a hefty woman in her sixties who screamed at us in Russian from the moment we entered at four p.m. till we left the next morning at ten. I have no idea why. It's just a fact of life in the former Soviet Union: Anyone over fifty working in the service industry shouldn't be in the service industry. This goes for hotel clerks, porters, waiters, flight attendants, and roadside fruit vendors. They learned their trade in an age where your choice was no choice and the customer was always wrong.

Dinner at the hotel was the worst part of a miserable stay. I'd believed that you could always order food in a foreign country – menus generally have pictures you can point to; even when they don't, they're all laid out the same way, with starters in the upper left hand corner, entrees in the middle, and desserts at the end. Not this menu. There were no pictures, no prices – just two solid pages of tiny Cyrillic writing. It may not have been a menu at all – it might have been a laminated excerpt from "The Brothers Karamazov." I tried to communicate with the Ogress, who was also our waitress and short order cook – a literal triple threat. I attempted to order an entrée in mime, by acting like a chicken; when that failed, I mooed like a cow. This actually seemed to amuse her briefly before she went back to screaming at me. Trembling, I pointed at some random words on the menu. She brought something out – we paid for it and ate it. It may have been food.

The next morning we headed another two hundred miles north to Kiev. This is a worldly and welcoming city – I was accosted in the town square by a man in a ratty Bart Simpson costume. And they really do eat Chicken Kiev in Kiev – it's a breaded chicken cutlet stuffed with an entire stick of butter. If Elvis had known about this dish, he'd have died even younger.

My wife and I visited Kiev's beautiful public park where, from a raised viewing platform, we could view the Promised Land: Chernobyl, just sixty miles to the north. The park also boasted several monumental sculptures of Scrat, the ugly rat-squirrel hybrid from the "Ice Age" cartoons who always wants his acorn but never quite gets it. I asked a Ukrainian woman why her people liked Scrat so much. She replied, "He teaches children that life is hopeless."

Scrat is also the first star that greets you when you enter my favorite Kiev attraction: the Muzeum of Wax Persons. Wax celebrities have careers just like professional baseball players – the very best wind up in the majors, the Madame Tussauds in large cities around the globe. When a star loses his luster through time (Arnold Schwarzenegger) or scandal (Arnold Schwarzenegger), he'll be sent off to the minors – small-town, off-brand wax museums. Arnold might even be painted green and presented as the Incredible Hulk. This kind of repurposing goes on all the time: Ellen Degeneres becomes David Spade becomes Billie Eilish. My friend swears he saw a wax James Madison, our shortest president, redressed as Peter Pan. To make things sadder, wax figures tend to turn brown over time, so that even a Gwyneth Paltrow will take on an Afro-Caribbean complexion. All these indignities were on display in Kiev's wax museum, filled with unrecognizable celebrities, shameless reworkings (the Cryptkeeper from "Tales from the Crypt" was dressed and labeled "Michael Jackson"), and weird cast-offs from other museums: the Freak who Could Fit a Videotape in His Mouth and the Man with the Really Bad Haircut. But my favorite attraction was not a wax figure, but a sign on the wall. Next to a sculpture that could have been any bald celebrity from Dwight Eisenhower to Charlie Brown, was a placard reading – and I'm quoting here verbatim:

"BRUCE WILLIS: From the middle of the eightieth years, Bruce tried to force one's way vainly through the upstairs. He had to play quite a bit by notable roles in the films of category of "B" and publicity rollers. He by chance was worn out in a studio tests in the 'pilot' issue of serial "Moonlight", after which he woke up a (star). And with an output on the screens of "Die hard" the career of Bruce Willis shot up to the extraordinary heights. Psychological thriller "Sixth sense" became one of cashdesk in America, comedy The whole Nine yards also declared itself not bad."

I was starting to love Ukraine – its beauty, its boobs, its booboos – when my travel agent called with bad news: Chernobyl would be closed for the month. It wasn't a safety issue – there was a property dispute with a farmer whose fields you had to cross to get to the power plant's wreckage. Plutonium did not rattle the tour operators half as much as an angry farmer with a pitchfork. (TRAVEL TIP: Don't buy produce from a farm next to Chernobyl. Unless you get a really good price.)

I had to break the news to my wife, the words no husband should ever have to say: "Honey, I can't take you to Chernobyl."

What followed was the second-biggest meltdown in Ukrainian history.

Here I push the button that would have destroyed New York.

This man's job was to launch nukes at America. All is forgiven.

My wife at the Muzeum of Wax Persons, between the guy with barbells on his nipples and the man with a videotape in his mouth.

Iceland Left Me Cold

It's one of the few facts we all remember from grade school: "Greenland is actually icy and Iceland is really green!" And like everything we learned in school, it's completely wrong. Thanks to climate change, Greenland is getting greener by the day. And Iceland is cold as crap. It's chilly in the summer and in the winter, only an idiot would go there.

I am that idiot.

My wife dragged me to Reykjavik in February to see the Northern Lights. You may recall we'd already gone to Alaska to see the lights and it was a frost-bitten disaster. But you know the saying: "Fool me once, shame on you. Fool me twice, blame the wife." We checked into a hotel that featured prime viewing of the aurora borealis. Every forty minutes, from two to eight in the morning, hotel workers would bang on our door shouting. "They're happening! They're happening!" We'd run out into the polar night, still in our pajamas, only to hear "You missed it! You missed it!"

We did catch a couple of good looks at the Northern Lights, and let me say something no one else has the courage to admit: They're a big, celestial nothin'. They look great in "National Geographic" because, by some cruel joke of a sadistic God, the Northern Lights photograph beautifully. Through my camera lens, I saw an electrical fireworks spectacular. To my naked eye, just wispy clouds of gray-green smoke.

The Northern Lights: gorgeous on camera, not much in person. Just like Julianne Moore. I saw her at the grocery store once.

Still the natural beauty of Iceland does not disappoint; there are massive caves of ice, frozen waterfalls, and squat, shaggy horses that resemble comedy writer Bruce Vilanch.

It all looks like something out of "The Lord of the Rings," and that's no coincidence: Peter Jackson scouted locations here that he duplicated in his fifty-seven-hour film trilogy. We took a nature walk there, and in true Tolkien fashion, the hike was led by a giant. He stood seven feet tall and was ninety percent beard. When we came to an icy river, he picked up my wife in his mighty arms and carried her across. And then, against my will, he did the same to me. Finally, in a truly surreal touch, he pulled out an accordion and played polka tunes atop a glacier. My first question was "Why?" My second question was "Where? Where the hell was this guy hiding an accordion on his person?" My guess? His butt.

There's so much more to see in Iceland. Actually, just three things.

There's Blue Lagoon, a huge spa warmed by geothermal energy and tourist pee. Each year, seven hundred thousand visitors (twice the population of Iceland!) come to soak in God's Jacuzzi. And since the waters are said to have healing powers, many, many of those tourists suffer from skin diseases like eczema. This is Iceland's number one attraction: a bubbling slow cooker jammed with thousands of people, most of them blistered, flaking, and oozing. I'd sooner share a toothbrush with Willie Nelson.

Iceland's most photographed site is Hallgrimur's Church. It resembles a stylized pair of praying hands, soaring hundreds of feet in the air, a stunning tribute to the power of faith and God's love.

And, it's within walking distance to the penis museum!

Yes, not far from the cathedral is the Icelandic Phallological Museum, a single tiny space crammed with hundreds of penises (again, like Bruce Vilanch). Twenty whale peckers cross overhead like rafters, while several more run from floor to ceiling; these are load-bearing wieners. My wife seemed particularly taken with a tanned walrus wang, which jutted out of the wall like an obscene water main. Feeling threatened, I kept trying to steer her toward a display of hamster penises, but she wasn't budging.

But we were there to see the Northern Lights. My wife rented a cabin deep in the heart of Iceland that was said to be ideal for night sky viewing. As we drove out of Reykjavik, we stopped at what should be a tourist spot, but isn't: the lone, unremarkable grave of Bobby Fischer. He'd been the greatest chess player who ever lived; then he went a little nutso, spent a dozen years as a fugitive, had all his dental fillings removed, and did some jail time in Japan. This world-famous Jewish kid from Brooklyn wound up in a small suburb of Reykjavik, buried in front of a tiny church. It was a surprising final move in the unorthodox endgame of Bobby Fischer.

We arrived at our cabin, which was miles from anything else in Iceland, which itself is miles from anything on earth. The owner was Dag, a Kenny Loggins-looking hippie who seemed unaware that being a hippie was no longer a thing. His previous houseguest had been Queen guitarist Brian May, who'd also come to see the aurora borealis. (Mr. May, like many rock musicians, has a doctorate in astrophysics.) Years later, I met Brian May and told him about this shared experience. Professor May immediately launched into a forty-minute lecture on the aurora borealis. That's when I whispered something to my wife I never thought I'd say: "Get me away from Brian May."

Dag served us a hearty stew of his own recipe, then led us outside to see the Northern Lights. There were none – the sky was as thickly clouded as it's ever been in human history. That's when Dag went a little nutso – he wandered into an icy lake up to his waist and tried to catch us some fish with his bare hands. Illuminated by the headlights of his Jeep, I realized how much Kenny Loggins resembled Charles Manson.

We returned to Dag's home empty-handed. We were a hundred miles from the nearest living soul, trapped in a cabin with a crazed, wet hippie. Our vacation had turned into a horror movie, and not a particularly good one. I was certain we'd wind up ingredients in the hearty stew Dag served his next guests.

The next morning rose bright and cloudy. Dag woke up chipper and full of hippie hope, determined to show us a good time. He set each of us on his prized snowmobiles and gave us the forty seconds

I pretend to understand Brian May's lecture on astronomy.

We shared our cabin in Iceland with a psychopath.

of training needed to master them. Only an idiot couldn't handle one.

I was that idiot.

I immediately got stuck in a patch of wet snow and started gunning the engine to escape. The snowmobile belched black smoke… then burst into flame.

"What did you… how did you…it's not possible!" Dag sputtered. In a country full of surreal sights this was the most Dali-esque: a mellow hippie completely losing his cool while a snowmobile blazed like a Yule log.

Who needs the Northern Lights?

Scandinavia in Four Baldwins

How do I describe the countries of Scandinavia to you? Sweden, Denmark, Norway, and the other one. So vast, so beautiful, all very similar, and yet… distinctively different. They're like… the four Baldwin Brothers: Alec Baldwin, Billy Baldwin, Steven Baldwin, and the other one. Like the Baldwins, the Scandinavian countries are all kind of handsome in the exact same way. And like the Baldwins, these nations are just a bunch of white folks.

Sweden is one of my favorite places, and Stockholm is the loveliest capital city on earth. Sweden is definitely Alec Baldwin – rich, thriving, and versatile. Alec is an Oscar nominee, an Emmy winner. He does drama, he does comedy, but even when he's being funny it's kind of serious, like he could punch you in the mouth at any moment. Sweden's like that, too. That's why they give out all the Nobel Prizes… except the Peace Prize. Peace looked at the Swedes and said, "Peace out. You can give ME in Norway."

Sweden did once have a brooding quality. It was said to have the world's highest suicide rate – but now it's fallen to number twenty-eight. Even America is beating it. USA! USA! Oh wait, that's a bad thing. Sweden was home to Ingmar Bergman, so just like Alec, it used to make great movies but not so much anymore. It's fat and happy, just like you-know-who.

Denmark is the Billy Baldwin of nations – solid, contented, prosperous. They'd both impress us, if we hadn't heard of Alec and Sweden. Billy gave us "Backdraft" and "Flatliners"; Denmark gave us Hans Christian Andersen and Tivoli Gardens, an amusement park that feels like Disneyland, if they'd stopped maintaining it back in 1958. Billy's been married to singer Chynna Phillips for twenty-five years, so both Billy and Denmark have solid relations with China. Wow, that's a stretch.

Stephen Baldwin is like Norway – you've heard of it, you know it's out there, you're just not sure what it does. Stephen made one great movie, "The Usual Suspects," and one great DVD, "Livin' It," a Christian skateboard video. Norway, too, has one great of everything. One great playwright – Ibsen. One great composer – Grieg. One great painter, Munch, who painted one great painting, "The Scream." Munch knew he had a winner here, so he painted it four different times, then did it in pen and ink, and finally as a lithograph. "The Scream" is just like "Scream," the movie: There's a couple of good ones and a bunch of bad sequels.

Norway also has one great sculptor, Gustav Vigeland, but he's a doozy. If you've never heard of him it's because he never allowed his work to leave the country. But Oslo's Frogner Park, and you gotta love that name, has two hundred and twelve Vigeland sculptures, and a monolith with another one hundred and twenty one figures on it. They're all weird. It's hard to pick a favorite, but I'm going with the fat naked guy being attacked by four flying babies.

Finally we come to Finland and Daniel Baldwin, proof that not every country and not every Baldwin has to be great. You've gotta feel for them, as they've both had long struggles: one with cocaine, the other with Russia. I won't say which has what problem, but in 1998, Daniel was busted for running naked through the Plaza Hotel shouting "Baldwin!" Similarly, Finland shouts "Finlandia," a symphonic piece of bombast by Sibelius. It's their one great cultural export.

Finland is a lovely green place, but there's not much to it. We booked a city tour of the capital, Helsinki, and one of the highlights was stopping at the river to watch women beat carpets. But Finland has one attraction that even out-weirds Frogner Park. I can't believe it exists, even after I visited it. There's a hollowed-out mountain above the Arctic Circle, built to serve as a fallout shelter in case there's another Chernobyl-type disaster. But the Finns hated to see it sitting empty, so they took this huge underground bunker, accessible only by a hundred-and-fifty foot-long tunnel and turned it into a Christmas Village. There's ice sculptures, a carousel, a kiddie coaster, and piped-in Christmas music. And at the heart of it all, Santa.

They really tried hard, but none of it makes you forget how claustrophobic the place is. If Dr. Strangelove had been a Christmas movie, it would have had a set like this. If Santa were a Bond villain, this would be his lair.

Oh, there's two Baldwin sisters, too. They don't act. Let's say they're Iceland and Greenland.

Santa Park is built in the core of this mountain.

Urinal, Puerto Vallarta, Mexico

SIDE TRIP: Toilets of The World

I'm going to start with an important bit of information, something no tour guide will ever tell you and no travel book will ever print. When you take a big trip, you don't poop. You'll pee, but you won't poop. If you're traveling with a group, no one in the group will poop.

Once you're aware of this, you can relax. You can even be smug about it. "Using the toilet? Oh, yes, that's something I used to do myself. Back in my younger days, of course."

In time, the problem corrects itself. Generally after six or seven days, when you've reached maximum storage capacity. Before you know it, you'll be crapping like a native. Bully for you!

But why does this even happen? According to Professor Ross E. Forp, the act of defecation puts you in a vulnerable position –your pants are down, you're squatting, and you're alone. You're an ideal target for predatory animals or hostile outsiders. So our hominid ancestors evolved to shut down the poop reflex whenever they found themselves in an unfamiliar land.

Actually, I made that all up. There is no Professor Ross E Forp – Ross E Forp is just "professor" spelled backwards. But I think it's a pretty good theory. And it is related to a genuine phenomenon, one I'm sure you've noticed: The sound of rushing water makes you pee. It's the reason Niagara Falls has more toilets than any other National Park: The sound of rushing water convinces your brain that other people are peeing around you. It's safe for you to do it too, and the sooner the better.

Once you're on vacation and it's "all systems go," heh-heh, you will need to use foreign toilets. Be warned that in Cuba, every toilet is broken. Every single one. The Cuban flag should have a broken toilet on it. They should put one on their money.

We were leaving a restaurant in Cuba when we spotted a busted toilet in the alley – cracked ceramic, large chunks missing, stripped of all its metal hardware. "There it is, honey," I told my wife. "The brokenest toilet in Cuba. So busted they finally threw it away."

She replied, "Or maybe they're getting ready to install it."

In Europe, you'll encounter a different obstacle – the bathroom attendant. This is a woman – it's always a woman, generally old and bitter at the hand life has dealt her. She guards the entrance to a public bathroom like a troll in a fairy tale. To get in, you have to give her a small local coin. If you don't have one, you must give her a large local coin – and they don't give change. Your money pays the salaries of the people who keep the bathroom clean. But once you get inside, you realize the bathroom is not clean. It's filthy and there are always several inches of water on the floor. Too late – you paid your money, no refunds. For an additional fee, you can also purchase toilet paper, because there's none in the bathroom. The bathroom attendant will dole that out in meager squares, as if she were dispensing original Lincoln letters.

And folks, you're still in Western society. Just wait till you get to the developing world. For most of the people on earth – North Africans, Middle Easterners, ALL OF ASIA – a toilet is just a ceramic hole in the ground. You straddle this thing, one foot on either side, standing on two corrugated bricks. These are like the starting blocks Olympic racers use, because once you're done, you want to sprint out of there like you were Usain Bolt. Once again, you'll find no toilet paper. Instead, your tiny stall will be crowded by a giant trashcan full of water, a garden hose with kitchen spray nozzle, and a plastic pitcher. I've used these toilets for years and have never figured out how all this equipment is supposed to work.

In Africa, you'll find abundant Western-style toilets. But no toilet seats. Even in the finest hotels, you'll see beautiful johns with brass fixtures and wood cabinetry – but no seats. It sounds like the plot of a just terrible thriller: Who is stealing the toilet seats of Africa? And how are they stealing them? Do they slip them under their clothes? Is this why they wear daishikis? And why are they stealing them? Is there a resale market? Who sells used toilet seats? And who would buy one? Maybe they steal them for personal use. But why? Did they buy a toilet that had no seat? Or did a friend steal theirs? And is that a friend you care to have?

So many questions. Africa, truly a land of mysteries.

When you do need a toilet overseas, it's very hard to ask for one. The British, who seem so refined, go right for it. "Where's the toilet, mate?" Good for them.

By the way, I used a public restroom in London, right across the street from Big Ben. As I entered, I saw a homeless man using the hot air hand dryer, to, well, blow his wiener. Several hours later, after a tour of Parliament, I went back to use that bathroom. My wife asked, "Was your friend in there?"

I said, "My friend?" Denise has a very loose sense of what constitutes male bonding.

ANYWAY. When I ask for a toilet overseas, I rely on American euphemisms. These completely baffle foreigners: the men's room. The restroom. The washroom. The bathroom. They all sound like great rooms, none of which contain toilets. And the line, "I need to use the little boy's room" makes you sound like Michael Jackson.

I've heard some great euphemisms over the years: "I have to pick some flowers." "I need to visit the old house down the lane." And my favorite, used by members of the French Resistance: "I have to telephone Hitler." By the way, in researching this – and I do research this – I learned that Hitler's toilet is now in New Jersey. Hasn't it suffered enough?

There will come times in your travels where the toilet is not just a convenience – it's a necessity. If you travel long enough, you will get sick with what my wife calls "tummy trouble." What she means is diarrhea, but I don't want to say that and you don't want to read it. So instead of saying diarrhea, I'll say…Diane Keaton.

The first time I got sick was in Tanzania. I have no idea what caused it – maybe it was that ice cube they put in my soda, or that baked potato I found on the sidewalk. It was in foil, people! Whatever the cause, I was suddenly overcome with Diane Keaton. My tour guide drove frantically through the countryside, trying to find medical help. Along the way, I made emergency stops wherever I could – gas stations, the middle of a corn field, and once – I'm not proud of this – in a half-finished building using a toilet that wasn't hooked up to anything. Eventually he got me to a medical clinic that had clearly been a bicycle shop in the not-too-distant past. A doctor quickly saw me and handed me a teeny tiny green pill. Within three minutes, I was completely cured. I don't just mean 'no more Diane Keaton' – I felt good enough to win the Indy 500, without a car. The cost of this doctor's appointment including medicine: seventy-two cents.

The next time I got sick, it was completely my fault. I was visiting Syria, a country known for the destruction and vast human toll of its civil war. But before that, it was the most welcoming place I'd ever been. Of the 134 countries I've been to, I found the Syrians the finest people on earth. I wish we could populate the planet with them.

I was so enamored of these people that I joined a group of strangers for dinner at a café. Then I started drinking water from a pitcher on the table. The Syrians tried to stop me, but I wouldn't listen. I was operating under the shaky logic that if the people are so nice, how bad could their water be? I drank the entire pitcher. If you're thinking I'm an idiot, well, you're right. I mean who else would vacation in Syria?

The next day, I discovered that the friendliness of the Syrians does not extend to the microbial level. I was racked with explosive Diane Keaton – I pooped all over the Roman ruins at Palmyra. These were a UNESCO World Heritage site. They were. Till I got there.

We were on a group tour of Thailand, when our guide pulled over to buy us a roadside treat: sticky rice. It's a mixture of white rice, milk, and sugar, all steamed inside a bamboo tube. It was delicious, but within hours, forty of us on the bus were afflicted with Diane Keaton, in an Oscar-worthy performance.

It hit me that night as we were strolling the streets of Chiang Mai. I started sweating profusely – I stripped off my shirt, something I never do in public and rarely do in private. Soon I became delirious, and everyone in Thailand became my friend. I began shaking hands with passing strangers, saying "What's up, Jar Jar? How you doin', Jar Jar?"

"Stop being charming!" my wife pleaded.

"I can't," I replied. Eventually Denise got me back to the hotel. Luckily, she had skipped the sticky rice. My wife watches what she eats and avoids carbs entirely. This has given her the trim figure of "Annie Hall" star Diarrhea.

WHERE BEER COMES FROM: Beer keg urinal, Northern Ireland.

Chapter 4

WHAT AM I DOING IN SOUTH AMERICA?

americans don't travel enough to South America, and that's a shame. It's RIGHT THERE. The name even gives you directions: Go South of America and you're in South America.

And you'll be glad you went. Ecuador feels like the most charming parts of Spain and just might have the best food in the world. Not bad for a country that only exists because an imaginary, invisible line passes through it.

And Buenos Aires is fast-paced and cosmopolitan. It's just like New York City… in the '70s. It's almost nostalgic, having to watch out for pickpockets and clutch your purse to your chest; there's trash in the streets and graffiti on the walls. Luckily, the prices are also from the '70s: You can get a steak as big as a sailboat for six dollars. A three-dollar cab ride will get you anywhere in town.

Medellin, Colombia, once the center of world's drug trade, is a dead-ringer for San Diego. "What about Pablo Escobar?" my friends shriek. Well, he's been dead for twenty-eight years. In fact, Escobar's home is now a tourist attraction. The scariest part of my visit was having Pablo's brother, who's the ticket-taker, pitch me a movie about his life. "I want to call it 'Escobar's Brother: The Devil's Accountant.' Benicio Del Toro could play me." The man looked nothing Benicio Del Toro.

While I was in Colombia, I asked a local woman, "Donde esta Starbucks?" She stuck her tongue out at me. I figured it was because I was asking for American coffee in a country that grows the world's best. But no, Colombians point with their tongues instead of their fingers. Weird. But charming.

Despite what you may think, South America is not a strange land of hostile climate and rampant crime.

Except for the next three stories I'm going to tell you.

How to Beat the High Costa Rica

To all my friends who told me to visit Costa Rica – you are no longer my friends.

From the dawn of time until 1986, few people lived in Costa Rica and nobody visited. Then, in 1987, it became a hub of ecotourism; to give you a taste of those times, that same year, the Number One movie star on earth was Steve Guttenberg. Today, more than a million Americans visit Costa Rica every year. The locals are warm and friendly – in fact, a little too warm and friendly. It's a nation of loud, laughing close-talkers – one tour guide got so close he seemed to want to crawl in my mouth. All the hotels and restaurants are just lovely. But make no mistake – it's a jungle out there.

And what is a jungle but ferns growing on trees, vines growing on ferns, and moss growing on vines. It's a dense chaos of green and it all looks the same: A five-mile hike in the north looks just like five one-mile hikes in the south. Werner Herzog, who made so many films set in the jungle, put it best:

"Nature here is violent. I would see fornication, and asphyxiation, and choking. And fighting for survival, and growing, and just rotting away." In case you didn't get the point, he added, with typical German light-heartedness, "The trees here are in misery. The birds are in misery. I don't think they sing, they just screech in pain."

This is what you go to Costa Rica to see. There are five hundred thousand different animal species in the country, but they all live in a jungle, with infinite places to hide. We hired a tracker to help us find them – his name was Diego, and he looked exactly like our driver who looked exactly like our hotel clerk, and they all looked just like Josh Gad. Because it is a small, closely-knit country, there's much less diversity among the people than the parrots. There are basically four different faces shared by all of Costa Rica's men (and at least a few of its women): Everyone looks like Josh Gad, Mario Lopez, Patton Oswalt, or Cheech. While it's an amazing cast for a sitcom, it's weird for a whole country. If Patton Oswalt ever robs a bank here, there will be at least one million suspects.

Diego, our tracker, led us through the jungle promising we might see monkeys and pumas and tapirs, oh my! For two hours, we saw nothing. Suddenly Diego froze in his tracks.

DIEGO: Look! Up in the tree!

ME: Which tree? Your entire country is a forest.

DIEGO: In the soncoya tree, behind the Pitanga tree behind the Palanga tree. Sixty feet up – it's a sloth!

ME: I couldn't see that if I was Superman.

Diego handed me some binoculars, and I finally made out a curled-up furry ball hanging from a branch. To me, it looked like the tree's testicle. To my wife, it was ADORABLE. Mind you, from a distance of four hundred yards, anything looks adorable. A hospital Dumpster. A burning schoolbus.

So the day wasn't a total loss, Diego trained his telescope on the top of another tree so we could see actual wildlife: a wild avocado. Holy guacamole.

We later learned there were many other things in that jungle we couldn't see: poisonous snakes, scorpions, tarantulas, and a tiny tree frog with enough venom to kill a thousand people. Who thought that was necessary? Who figured a bite-size frog could have so many enemies? Even smaller and harder to avoid were the army ants. They lock onto you with their poison pincers then send out a pheromone message to their billion brothers: "Hey, get over here and let's eat this guy!"

It's not just the little things you can't see in Costa Rica – there are big things too, like a volcano. Mount Arenal is one of the top natural wonders in the country, but it's perpetually blanketed in fog. Diego raved about it:

DIEGO: When the sky is clear, you can see the volcano for forty kilometers in every direction.

ME: Is it beautiful?

DIEGO: I don't know. I've never seen it.

He then added, somewhat unnecessarily, "You couldn't see it even before Covid."

It made you wonder if there was even a volcano there at all. Perhaps a couple of entrepreneurs collected all the fog machines from Costa Rica's bankrupt discos and piled them up in one place. They had created a permanent cloud bank, but what could they do with it?

ENTREPRENEUR #1: We could tell people there's a mountain under it.

ENTREPRENEUR #2: Too boring.

ENTREPRENEUR #1: How about a dragon?

ENTREPRENEUR #2: Too crazy.

ENTREPRENEUR #1: How about a volcano?

ENTREPRENEUR #1: Bueno! That's like a mountain version of a dragon.

A second tour guide, also named Diego, also resembling Josh Gad, led us on another hike. It was three hours straight up a muddy mountain, to see Mistico, "the river with blue water."

"But Mike," you may be asking, "isn't all water blue?"

YES!!!!!!

For the entire hike, Diego 2 berated me for the things I didn't bring:

"You no bring mosquito repellent?"

"You no bring binoculars?"

"You no bring hiking boots?"

"You no bring lunch?"

"You no bring horsefly spray?"

First of all, is that even a thing? Second, as a tour guide maybe he could have told me what to bring IN ADVANCE. Of course, if I had, I'd be lugging about two hundred pounds of stuff straight up a mountain.

We reached the summit, which would have been a perfect spot to see "the river with the blue water," except the valley was covered in fog. So Diego Dos, as the locals might call him, launched into a lengthy lecture on the difference between moss and lichen. All at once, the clouds opened up with a rainstorm of Biblical proportions. Diego 2 ignored it, continuing on with this lecture nobody asked for. The one thing he never said to me was, "You no bring umbrella?" because Costa Ricans aren't bothered by rain. They, like fish, are not actually aware they're wet. He finished his speech, and noticed I was now drenched to the skin. He said, "Man, you sure sweat a lot."

And this is an important fact that nobody tells you about Costa Rica: It never stops raining.

Sometimes it's a drizzle, sometimes it's a downpour, and there's a once-in-a-century flood twice every week. The only wetter country on earth is Atlantis.

It's called a tropical rainforest, but that's burying the lead: It should be called a rainy tropical rain forest where it rains all the goddam time. This is why you never see the wildlife here: because every animal knows to go for cover when it rains. Every animal, that is, except the Costa Rican tourist: Boobus costaricus.

"I thought this was the dry season!" I raged at one of the Diegos.

"It is the dry season. We get a lot of rain during the dry season."

"Well, when do you get the least rain?" I asked.

"During the rainy season."

Besides the rainforest, Costa Rica has a cloud forest, because all their forests have bad weather. There's also a tropical dry forest, but my guide assured me, "It rains a lot there."

My wife and I got back to the hotel that night and hung all our wet clothes out to dry. The next morning, we were surprised to learn that our wet clothes were even wetter. And they stank.

"You stink," my wife told me.

"You stink," I replied.

It was like a grade school production of "Who's Afraid of Virginia Woolf?"

The damp had permeated everything. Our dry clothes were now wet. Money turned to mush. Envelopes sealed themselves. Extra Crunchy Cheetos became regular Cheetos.

I tried going out in a rain poncho, but hiking in the tropics while sealed into non-breathable plastic tends to cook one alive. I actually smelled like the Swanson's Boil-in-Bag Chicken A La King Dinners my mother slowly poisoned me with as a child. (Nowadays they call this cooking sous vide and charge eighty bucks a plate for it.)

So that was my vacation— two weeks slogging through the jungle in pouring rain, seeing less wildlife than I do on an average New York subway ride. Rats are wildlife, right?

I hated Costa Rica. So why do millions of Americans say they love it?

Maybe they won't admit they spent precious time, and even more precious money, on a trip they didn't like. I don't have that problem. I'm willing to say the things no one else will admit: "Ghostbusters" isn't funny; "Mad Men" was boring; chocolate lava cake is not worth the wait. My motto is, "If you don't have something bad to say, don't say anything at all."

Or maybe it's the Wayne Newton Syndrome. I've been told that Wayne Newton was a masterful entertainer in his time. In my time, he's kind of sucked, putting on a lousy Vegas show night after night for decades. Audiences walk out disappointed but saying, "I heard he was good last night." Maybe Costa Rica is the Wayne Newton of Central American countries – there's a slogan! You get rained on for a week, but you tell yourself, "I heard it was sunny last week."

Even I will admit there are some nice things about Costa Rica:

- The hot springs of Tabacon – a dozen warm-water pools, each one unique – is a perfect blending of nature and design.
- Drinking water is free in restaurants, something you don't find anywhere outside the US.
- You'll see six or seven rainbows every day.

Basically, if there's anything good about having way too much water, you'll find it in Costa Rica. And I've been told the country's Nicoya Peninsula is warm and dry. But Mel Gibson lives there, so, ick.

Blame it on Rio

I once had a new boss who invited me to his home for dinner. When I arrived at the appointed time, my boss had completely forgotten who I was and why I'd come to his home. He and his wife were in their underwear, watching TV, and eating take-out. They stared at me like I was a crazy stranger who dropped into random homes looking for free meals. I slowly backed out and, in the thirty years I worked with this man, I've never mentioned it again.

Rio de Janeiro is like my boss.

In 2017, 6.6 million people visited Rio and the city wasn't ready for any of them. There are no information stands, no tourist centers, no currency exchanges. No one speaks English – they don't even speak Spanish! Brazilians speak Portuguese, a language spoken outside of Brazil by one-sixth of one percent of the world's population. Even other South Americans visiting Rio are out of luck.

This is not to say Rio de Janeiro is not the worst place on earth. (Honduras is.)

But Rio is the worst place on earth that you think is going to be fun. (Grandma's house is a close second.) It looks great in the movies. There's that giant Christ the Redeemer statue on top of a mountain. Only it's not all that giant – you've seen bigger figures inflated on top of car dealerships. It's made of poured concrete and is about the blandest looking Jesus you'll ever see. The name is a tip-off – Christ the Redeemer? You can just picture this Savior sitting home clipping coupons.

Nearby is Rio's other major tourist disappointment – a mountain called Sugarloaf. A sugarloaf is a lump of sugar shaped like a mountain. So, despite its colorful name, Sugarloaf is basically a mountain shaped like a mountain.

What was I doing here?

My wife and I had come to Rio for Carnivale, that glittering fiesta of massive debauchery. I'd expected it to be spilling out into the streets, with parties and parades everywhere, like Mardi Gras in New Orleans. But Carnivale is a private ticketed event, held in a special stadium. Outside that arena, you'd have no clue anything was happening.

There were signs for a "Celebration in the Park," but, in typical Rio fashion, the organizers lost interest once the signs were posted. Hundreds of angry tourists showed up for what should have been called Nothing in the Park. As I fought my way through the crowd, I got squashed up against a ferocious-looking woman. I apologized; she snarled back. It was only when I emerged from the mob that I realized she had torn the pocket off my pants and taken all the money I had.

I walked ten feet to a policeman who was sunning himself on the hood of his patrol car. He was actually using a tanning reflector, something I'd only seen as a prop in '60s bikini comedies. I told the cop I'd just been robbed. He looked at me, baffled: Did I know him? Were we friends? Why was I bothering him with my problems?

"She's still there!" I said, pointing to her. "The black woman. The really ugly one!"

"They are all ugly," he said and went back to tanning. Not just a lousy cop, a racist, too. I hope he got melanoma.

I'd been to over a hundred countries, many of them hellholes, some of them war zones. But this was the first time I'd ever gotten robbed. The second time, actually – the first was two hours before. I put my bankcard in a Rio ATM, and heard it fall with a plunk, like a coin in a piggy bank. I pushed every button on the machine but nothing happened. I picked up the emergency phone to report it, but that was broken, too. Finally, I wailed on the machine with both fists, till the front flipped open. Kids, violence solves everything!

The ATM had been completely gutted, and there was a pile of bankcards sitting inside it. Apparently, crooks would come by every couple of hours to harvest the cards. Luckily, I took my ATM card back. I took everyone else's card, too. Right now, I'm typing this on a laptop purchased with the AmEx of Mrs. Lisa Lavoie. Lisa, if you're out there reading this, thank you.

Crime, of course, is the one area where Rio really delivers. The city's wealthy tourist area is surrounded by favelas, a ring of shanty towns up in the hills. The Brazilians handled this problem the best way they know: cosmetic surgery. They painted the slums in bright day-glo colors. They're still a nest of poverty and hopelessness, but now they look like a package of Starburst candies. Problem solved. They even give walking tours of the favelas. "The people here are very poor, but they never steal from each other," chirped our guide. "We steal from you – the tourists! How many of you have been robbed since you got here?" There were twelve of us in the group – eight raised their hands.

There was no escape from crime, even at a costume contest we attended. There were women in elaborate confections of feathers and spangles. One guy came as Big Ben (he was, in fact, the only clock in Rio keeping correct time). Another was dressed as the entire city of San Francisco, with glittering lights and moving cable cars.

And the winner was… a woman (or possibly a man) dressed as Evita. S/he wore a white dress and had blonde hair. That's it. The judges had clearly been bribed and the crowd knew it. The fancy dress ball ended in violence. You can't spell "riot" without R-I-O.

EXPLOSIVO

What kind of diarrhea did I get in Rio?

But the real costume ball in town was Carnivale – it's a non-stop parade that lasts from nine p.m. till dawn, two nights in a row. I missed the first evening, having caught a terrible stomach ailment from something I ate. Or touched. Or looked at. I sent my wife off alone, at night, into a strange and truly dangerous city. (I'm a great husband.) I stayed in bed, shivering, sweating, and watching TV. The only thing on was "Suddenly Susan," dubbed into Portuguese. If you don't remember this show, it was a Brooke Shields sitcom based on the premise that there's nothing remotely funny about Brooke Shields. When that episode ended, another "Suddenly Susan" began. I scrambled for the remote, but it squirted from my sweaty hand and rolled under the bed. I was too wracked with chills to get it, so I lay there all night, watching a "Suddenly Susan" marathon. The only thing worse than watching six hours of this show in Portuguese would have been watching it in English.

I dragged myself out of bed for the second and final night of Carnivale. Thousands of Brazilians participate, representing dozens of Rio neighborhoods. Every group dances to its own special samba, and every samba sounds exactly the same. Their outfits all look similar too – giant contraptions of Mylar, plumes, and sequins. It's like a massive invasion from the planet Fabulous.

Carnivale costumes can cost up to fifty thousand dollars each, and the poor people of Rio pay for it themselves. What could have been their child's college education is spent on an outfit they wear once, as they swagger down the mile-long promenade. When they reach the end, they throw it away, right where they're standing. From glamor to garbage in five seconds. By sunrise, several city blocks were piled high with spangled headdresses and feathered brassieres.

It was surreal.

It was also the greatest show I'd ever seen in my life. Carnivale was worth all my suffering: the robberies, the diarrhea, the rigged costume ball, and the twelve episodes of "Suddenly Susan." I was hooked, so I came back to Rio for the 2016 Olympics.

Once again, the city invited the world to a party they forgot they were throwing. They'd had four years to plan, but seemed to throw it all together in the last couple of days. Many venues were unfinished; others were visibly crumbling while the events took place. Spectators agree it was the worst Olympics of the past, say, three thousand years.

Oh, and I got robbed again.

Have It Uruguay...

It would be the worst Jan and Dean song ever: "Four cows for every boy…" But there truly are 3.8 cows for every person in Uruguay. And due to proximity (or perhaps inter-breeding), the Uruguayans are somewhat bovine: stocky, slow-moving, quiet, and very contented. In fact, Uruguay has repeatedly been named "The Happiest Country in South America." I was skeptical – after all, Disneyland is called "The Happiest Place on Earth," and it's depressing and expensive and been home to eight accidental deaths and one murder.

My suspicions were aroused when we landed in the nation's capital, Montevideo. It is the rare large city with no nice parts whatsoever. If we have a romantic vision of this place, it's because we mispronounce it with flair: "Monta-vi-DAY-o." The locals pronounce it "Monty Video," making it sound more like an '80s shop where a guy named Monty rents VHS tapes. Mostly porn.

The city is bisected by a pedestrian mall that extends for miles – but I never saw any pedestrians because it wasn't much of a mall. No restaurants, no shops, no video rental… just shuttered storefronts, graffiti, and bird crap. So much bird crap. At the end of the mall, I saw two homeless men cooking a steak over a cinderblock stuffed with newspaper. Uruguayans are the MacGyvers of grilling – they can fashion a barbecue out of anything: a broken bottle, a postage stamp, a block of ice. One of the dust-caked men offered me a hunk of their meat wrapped in a kitchen sponge. I took it – again, there were no restaurants around – and it was the greatest steak I ever ate in my life. And not great in the sense that "these poor men shared their meager meal with a total stranger in an act of true Christian charity." No – this was just a great-ass steak! When the cows outnumber the people four to one, there's no excuse for bad beef.

Steak is the main ingredient in the country's national dish, the chivito. It's a sandwich on French bread stuffed with an entire friggin' steak, as well as mozzarella, tomatoes, mayonnaise, black olives, green olives, and bacon. Oh, and ham, too – that's right, it's got two kinds of pork. And in case all that doesn't kill you, it's topped with a fried egg. It's a sandwich designed by committee – everyone in Uruguay chose an ingredient, and all of them went in. The finished chivito is about the size of a piece of carry-on luggage, and costs around three bucks. That includes a side of fries so huge, it seems they've brought you every French fry on earth. The chivito is sold everywhere, from drugstores to fine restaurants, and everyone eats them completely – I watched small children devour sandwiches larger than themselves.

The locals wash down this Tyrannosandwich Rex with a drink just as unique: mata. Every Uruguayan walks the streets encumbered with a pouch of mata leaves, a thermos filled with hot water, a coconut-shaped drinking vessel, and a silver drinking straw. Mata looks like tea, has the kick of coffee, and is as complex to prepare as crystal meth. You pack the leaves in the coconut, pour a splash of hot water over it, and sip it slowly over the course of the day. I liked the stuff so much, I brought home a whole mata rig and five pounds of leaves. Years later, it sits unopened in my cupboard.

The number one tourist destination in Uruguay is Punta del Este, a spit of land that curls into the Atlantic, and comes to a point so sharp you could cut a chivito with it. Both sides of the peninsula are developed with high-rise beach resorts, but there's a catch: On the sheltered bay side, the weather is calm and warm; on the ocean side, you're perpetually battered by cold ocean winds. Can you guess on which side Mr. Trump built his luxury condos? Here's a hint – the sign featuring Eric Trump has blown down and splintered to bits. You have to wonder about the quality of the

condo construction when even the billboard can't stand up. On the town's main beach stands the symbol of Punta del Este: a sculpture of five corpse-gray fingers, each the size of a man, clawing their way out of the sand. What does it even mean? "Come for a day at the beach – and get crushed by a giant from Hell!"

I left town via the only bridge – it has four, huge, nausea-inducing humps in it for no good reason – and headed to Atlantida, a city comprised entirely of quirk. I passed by a house that looks like an eagle, a hotel that looks like a ship, and a church that looks like an army of ice cream cones – all within a mile. They weren't tourist attractions and no one else seemed to notice them. I also visited the ruins of a castle inhabited by an alchemist… in 1966. Yes, they had a guy making a good living at alchemy there in the mid-sixties.

I reached my quirk quota, and then some, at a Uruguayan boutique hotel. It had no room numbers – just an abstract symbol on each door. This is fine until you get lost, which I did almost immediately. I spent three hours roaming the halls – was I in Zigzag or Squiggle? Spiral or Counterclockwise Spiral?

When I finally found my room, it was so crammed with idiosyncratic knick-knacks, there was no place for my bags. "Where can I put my luggage?" I asked the manager.

"Lug-gage?" he asked. Thirty years in the hotel business and he'd never encountered this concept.

I'd had enough. I wanted to go home to New York, where my house was shaped like a house and the number on the door was a number. This place was nice for awhile, but I finally got sick of its cuteness.

Just like Disneyland.

Nobody promised me Uruguay would be beautiful, or exciting, or fascinating. They didn't even say I'd be happy there – just that the locals were. I didn't quite get this till I met the happiest man in New York. He wasn't a mayor or a mogul or a movie star – he was a shabby guy on the subway gibbering gleefully on his cell phone: "I'm just swimming along, singing a song! Got a couple of lampreys hanging off my belly and some barnacles on my tail. But life is good, man! Life. Is. Good!"

It took me a moment to realize three things about this guy:

1. His cell phone was a baby shoe.

2. He thought he was a whale.

3. He was proud to be a whale, even if he really wasn't one.

Uruguay is like that. It's a nation of four million kooks who are inordinately proud of their country for no good reason. They're proud of their bizcochos, the national dessert that's just salty crumbs held together with grease. And they choke these down with their local coffee, which may be the worst in the world.   They've built gorgeous museums honoring their two best-known painters no one has ever heard of: Joaquin Torres Garcia (who draws like a child who owns four crayons) and Carlos Paez Villaro (who draws like Joaquin Torres Garcia). Uruguay really was a nice place to visit if you just lowered your standards enough.

Just like Disneyland.

SIDE TRIP: Don't Forget to Tip... and Tip... and Tip

Here's my favorite rule of thumb about travel: "Bring half the clothes and twice the money."

An even better rule might be, "Bring a quarter the clothes and four times the money."

But the best rule is probably, "Bring one change of clothes and a suitcase full of money." This, by the way, is how Russians travel, visiting foreign countries with luggage full of cash. A souvenir vendor in Turkey told me they compete to see who can gouge the Russians for the most money.

On a side note, never buy souvenirs. Your kids don't want them and your friends don't want them – "Here's a keepsake from a trip I took and YOU didn't." And if you buy something for yourself, by the time you get home, even you don't want it. A souvenir is like a Porsche – it loses sixty percent of its sentimental value as soon as you take it off the lot.

Even if you avoid souvenirs, you still have to pay for tour guides, great museums, horrible folklore shows, and that old devil, miscellaneous. Once I was crossing the border into the Congo, and a security guard told me I needed an unexpected visa. The cost? Three hundred eighty seven dollars. Cash.

It was exactly the amount of money I had in my pocket. How did she know?

Another friend of mine booked a villa in Venice for a month. At the end of the first week, he sent out a small bag of laundry. It came back with a bill for one thousand dollars. Both he and his shirts had been taken to the cleaners.

He spent the rest of the month washing his own clothes in the sink. He told me, "I found this wonderful stuff called Woolite. Have you ever heard of it? Woolite?" Any time I asked him about the magic of Venice, he'd just gush about the wonders of Woolite.

This man is a billionaire, by the way.

You'll need local currency in any place you visit. But foreign exchange bureaus can be enormously picky. In Myanmar, they refused half my money because the bills were nicked or creased. In return, they gave me currency that was ripped and faded, and one bill was held together with a Band-Aid. Still, it was fun, because their money is as big as a Pop-Tart, and one US dollar bill gets you one thousand, two hundred eighty-eight of theirs.

Excluding places like Myanmar, here's a handy tip for converting foreign prices to American: One of theirs equals one of ours. One euro equals one dollar. One British pound equals one dollar. A Canadian dollar equals a buck. This trick works great in India, Panama, Singapore, and Argentina. Some countries this doesn't work at all. Who cares? Do you want to do a bunch of algebra every time you buy a beer?

You can avoid exchange bureaus altogether. The good news is every country has ATMs. The bad news is they're all broken.

Even when they do work, ATMs only give out big bills. And no one in any third world country has change. If you have a foreign twenty dollar bill, it might as well be a million dollar bill. No one can break it. In India, I tried to buy one dollar's worth of aspirin with an Indian five-dollar bill. The pharmacist looked at it, screamed, and ran out of his own store. THIS REALLY HAPPENED! The man was a Hindu and he knew that in ten lifetimes he'd never be able to break a five.

And if you do manage to get small bills, they will be siphoned off you immediately. How? Tips. Tips! When you're on vacation, every day is a holiday known as Extended Palm Sunday. Wow, that's a bad joke!

One morning I was leaving Cairo to fly to Luxor, Egypt. I had to tip the hotel maid, the guy who brought my bag down to the lobby, the guy who brought my bag out to the cabstand, the guy who hailed the cab which was sitting right there, the cabbie, and the two men who grabbed my bag out of the car and wheeled it to airport security. Yes, it now took two men to handle the bag one man carried before – it had somehow doubled in weight during the ride over. I'd already tipped seven people before the sun even came up. And soon I'd be in Luxor, where the whole cycle would start all over again.

As my bag went through the X-ray machine, the Security Guy looked at me expectantly.

"You don't tip the luggage screening guy!" I shouted.

He shrugged. It was worth a try.

The biggest tip I'd ever been hit for came at fifteen thousand feet. Denise and I were four days into our climb up Mount Kilimanjaro, the fiasco which ends this book. As I was drifting off to sleep in our tent, Denise said, "I hope you have nine hundred dollars to tip the porters." I did not have nine hundred dollars cash. I would not carry nine hundred dollars cash if I were going on a world tour of strip clubs. I climbed the rest of Kilimanjaro knowing that at the end of the trip I'd be stiffing our ten burly porters. My plan was to reach the top of the mountain, jump off, and plunge to my death.

Tipping is not universal, by the way. Japan doesn't have it. Neither does Australia. I remember an elderly Australian woman telling me a horror story from her youth. "I was working as a chambermaid, and after I cleaned this woman's room, she gave me two pounds." The old lady shuddered. That was the whole story – someone tipped her. That was her Stephen King twist.

So trust me, my complaint with tipping is not the money. It's the aggravation. And the money. But mostly it's the aggravation.

And the money.

Chapter 5

YOUR DIRTY MOTHER: NATURE

The Serengeti

Zoos used to be POW camps for animals. They'd been captured and thrown in tiny bare cages, where they would die of despair. Our parents brought us to these places. For fun.

Today zoos are much more humane. They build their animals enormous enclosures filled with greenery for them to hide behind. As a result, you can spend all day (and seventy-one dollars) at the San Diego Zoo and not see one goddam animal.

Frankly, this is what I figured an African safari would be like. You'd see a giraffe every other day, and maybe one wildebeest. Whatever a wildebeest is.

But within one hour of pulling into Masai Mara Animal Reserve in Kenya, I saw tons of elephants, hundreds of hippos, a gazillion gazelles, an alliteration of antelopes, and wayyyy too many zebras. Africa has zebras like New York has pigeons. You see thousands of zebras in herd after herd. In their black-and-white stripes they look like a prison gang from a '30s movie that's up to no good.

And I saw literally millions of wildebeests. These animals survive and proliferate because they're ugly. No hunter wants to kill them. No one wants their ugly head mounted on a wall. It looks like a meat loaf with horns.

There's not only a lot of animals, but they're all friends. In the zoo, they're segregated by species, but in Africa, they hang out together, a bunch of smug, self-satisfied vegans. They truly are a peaceable kingdom, united by a common belief: Lions suck. Lions are the jerks of the jungle – eating you, eating your friends, ruining everyone's good time.

And yet, the highlight of any safari is to see a lion make a kill. The tough part is lions sleep all day, and eat all night, like your children coming home from college. My wife got us up at four a.m. to see lions on the hunt. It excited a bloodlust in her that I hadn't seen in thirty-four years of marriage:

MIKE: Hey honey, look, a warthog.

DENISE: He's so cute. He's like Poomba. Hi Poomba.

MIKE: Uh-oh, here comes a lion.

DENISE: KILL HIM! EAT HIM! KILL POOMBA!

MIKE: He's getting away.

DENISE: Dammit!

The only feeding we saw that morning was a hornbill eating some elephant dung. It was less "Lion King" than "Pink Flamingos."

A safari is one of the few vacations I recommend to everyone. For a reasonable price, you can even go glamping, where they build a Hilton Hotel room and throw a tent over it. I thought it was purely a gimmick, until I was kept awake one night by an elephant flossing his butt on our tent ropes. The accommodations are plush, the food is great, and the driving is a teeth-rattlling nightmare. You ride in a Jeep over the worst dirt roads on earth. There are seat belts, but they are purely decorative: The sliding part doesn't slide

and the buckle doesn't buckle. They are there for you to sit on, making an uncomfortable ride even more uncomfortable. Still it's worth it to see animals like the baboons, because they seem to be on safari, too. While you're watching baboons, they sit there quietly watching a bunch of lower apes screeching and screwing and throwing each other out of trees. For baboons, this was television. This was their "Schitt's Creek."

Here's another fun fact about baboons: If a man yells at them, they run away. If a woman yells at them, they don't listen. Baboons are like Republican senators: They cannot hear women.

Once you've seen all the big animals, you can go in search of the smaller, more obscure ones, turning your safari into a weeklong game of Where's Waldo? This will almost always lead to stress because in every couple, one person is a much better spotter:

DENISE: Look honey, a dik-dik.

MIKE: Where?

DENISE: You see where I'm pointing?

MIKE: What you see that you're pointing at is totally different from what I see you pointing at. It's called parallax…

DENISE (CONTROLLED RAGE): The dik-dik. Is right. There.

MIKE: Oh, now I think I see it. It's beautiful.

DENISE: Good.

MIKE: I like those bright red tail feathers.

DENISE: A dik-dik is a deer!'

And… fight.

Indonesia

Indonesia is the biggest Muslim country on earth, but it wears its religion lightly. If you visit the capital city of Jakarta, you'll see more bikinis than burqas, and more martinis than mosques. But mostly you won't see anything, because you can't move – Jakarta has the second worst traffic on earth – only Cairo is worse. The Egyptian government hired Japanese civil engineers to fix this problem, and after eighteen months they issued this report: "Nothing can be done."

In Jakarta, my driver picked us up at nine a.m. Over the next two hours, we moved three blocks. Three blocks! I asked the driver how he even managed to get to my hotel by nine.

"I left home at four this morning." He didn't even think it was weird.

The problem will only get worse, as climate change has caused repeated flooding of the city. But the government was quick to react: They moved the national capital to East Kalimantan, seven hundred miles away. If you're a politician, problem solved. If you're one of ten million people living in Jakarta, you will drown, while sitting in traffic.

But Indonesians are great at rolling with these things. Periodically one of their villages is swallowed up by an enormous sinkhole. We visited one – most of the residents moved on, but a few remained, giving motorcycle tours of the hole where their town used to be.

We ride around the sinkhole that, a week before, was this guy's village.

We'd gone to Indonesia for ecotourism. This is when you find an animal deep in the jungle, build a bunch of hotels around it, and tromp thousands of tourists through its once-secluded home. You are not so much saving the animal as turning it into a neurotic mess. You are making it a New Yorker.

But it's fun for the tourist. And perhaps by treasuring these animals, we're not inclined to eat them. That's why we have panda sanctuaries rather than panda burger franchises. Although what is in those dumplings from Panda Express? Nobody knows…

The problem with wildlife viewing is that animals choose to live in such inconvenient places. Once you're in Indonesia, you have to go to Borneo to see orangutans, fly to Sumatra to see tigers, and then sail to Komodo Island to see – come on, you know – Komodo dragons.

"If only you could gather these animals into one place where you could see them all at once," I said.

"That's called a zoo," replied my wife.

Visiting wildlife, like dying, has five steps. They are:

Step 1. Where is it?

Step 2. There it is!

Step 3. There's another one!

Step 4. God! There's like fifty of them.

Step 5. Okay, I've seen enough.

With animals, no matter how exotic, if you've seen one, you've seen them all. Animals of a species are all the same and they do the same damn thing over and over. They're not like Meryl Streep movies, where she does something different every time. They're like Adam Sandler movies.

The other problem with ecotourism is that while you're visiting the animals' habitats, they're visiting yours. We hiked through the jungles of Borneo looking for orangutans, only to find them hanging out by the ranger station, listening to his radio. They liked Eminem.

I walked all over bone-dry Komodo Island on a quest to find a dragon. I finally tripped over one on my way to the bathroom – he was lying out by the men's room steps enjoying the one piece of shade on the island. This could have been deadly, by the way. Komodos have a lethal bite, and it's a sloooow death due to all the bacteria in their teeth. They have the filthiest mouths this side of

Sarah Silverman.

Another problem is that the smarter animals learn our ways so quickly. In Uganda, we went into the woods looking for chimpanzees – the law allowed us to spend one hour with the chimps from

the moment we spotted them. But the chimps spotted us first, headed for the nearest clearing, and sat down. We followed – they had tricked us into getting the hell out of their forest. We watched them for awhile, snapping photos of them doing absolutely nothing. Suddenly, they all got up and left. I looked at my watch – it had been one hour exactly, and they knew it. Their time was up and they were punching out for the day.

It was a little disappointing. In fact, my fondest memory of this trip was our guide Kevin. He had four sons: Devon, Evan, Calvin, and Melvin.

"Are you going to have any more kids?" I asked.

He said, "I can't. I ran out of –Vin names."

In Rwanda, we slashed our way through the jungle looking for silverback gorillas. I was walking down the narrow trail when the guy behind rudely shoved me aside. I turned to yell at him and saw he was a gorilla. We'd cleared a nice path – he figured he'd use it.

It's not always this easy. In Indonesia, we took a plane to another plane, to a cab, to a Jeep, to see tigers in Sumatra. Our guide picked us up at ten a.m. By ten-fifteen, we were in the jungle sitting on a wooden platform high up in a tree. Eight hours later, we were still sitting there – no tigers.

"Are we going to see them?" Denise asked.

Our guide replied, "Oh no. They never come out after six in the morning."

"Then why did you pick us up at ten?"

"I thought you wanted to sleep in."

We demanded the guide come back for us the next morning – early. He did, and we sat in that goddam tree again, from five in the morning till five in the afternoon. Again – no tigers.

I asked, "Just how often do you see tigers here?"

He replied, "Three times in the past fifteen years."

We had a better chance of seeing a comet. People in New Hampshire saw JD Salinger more than the Sumatrans saw tigers.

So that was my ecotourism in Indonesia: I stepped on a Komodo, missed the orangutans, and never had a shot of seeing a tiger. I didn't get a genuine animal experience till we traveled to Sulawesi. This is an Indonesian island almost certainly created by aliens. It looks like nothing else on the globe. Sulawesi is shaped like an end table brandishing a whip. It looks like a chai – that Hebrew symbol for life that was worn as a necklace by everyone in the '70s except Jews.

Things get weirder when you get to Sulawesi, because everyone lives in a house shaped like a canoe. Not just people: Pigpens, chicken coops, and doghouses all swoosh to a point on each side like a boat that doesn't float and won't go anywhere. Why do they do this? ALIENS!!!

Still, things seemed surprisingly normal when we were invited to a Sulawesi picnic. Locals wore their Sunday best – dresses, coats, and ties – and picnic lunches were spread out on the edges of an open field. At the center, ten water buffalo grazed peacefully. You see water buffalo all over Indonesia – they look like the love child of a cow and a hippo: fat, smooth, gray, and shiny. They are so docile, a six-year-old can move herds of them with a stick. The picnic looked like an Indonesian production of "Our Town."

And then the slaughter began.

A local man, possibly the mayor, cut the throat of one water buffalo. As the animal bled out, it looked more shocked than hurt: "Why'd you do that, man? I thought we were friends."

And here's the amazing part. As all this was going on, the other nine water buffalo just stood there, chewing their cud. They seemed to be saying, "Poor Fred. I sure hope that never happens to me."

But of course, it did happen to them. One by one the buffalo were killed, and six of the ten charged into the crowd, spraying blood like lawn sprinklers. The Sulawesi parents moved picnic baskets out of the charging animal's path; the kids just laughed. Meanwhile their fellow buffalo calmly watched their friends die like it was Netflix.

And then there were none. And as happy families looked on, all ten buffalo were butchered – from housepet to lunchmeat in under an hour. Everyone at the picnic got to go home with a door prize: a side of beef, a rack of ribs, enough steaks for a year.

"What the hell was that?" my wife asked. We couldn't believe our eyes, but we caught the whole thing on film.

We thought we'd seen something truly unique. Then we went to post it on YouTube, and found fifty videos just like ours. In Sulawesi, they do this every week, and every week, more than half the buffalo get loose. Wounded animals with horns six feet wide charge into crowds of families; yet no one ever thinks, "Maybe we should put up a fence. Maybe we should tie these animals to something."

To us, it was carnage and bloodshed and unchecked madness. To the people of Sulawesi, it was Sunday.

Sulawesi picnic: before and after.

The Galapagos

If you really want to see nature, lots of nature, way too much friggin' nature, I recommend a trip to the Galapagos. There's no restaurants, no hotels, no bars, no museums – you just look at the fish and the birds and the animals and the rocks.   Charles Darwin spent five weeks there and discovered Darwinism – but who wouldn't?

DARWIN: Everywhere you look, the same goddam finches on every bloody island. I mean, each island is slightly different, so the finches evolved to better adapt and HEYYYY…

The Galapagos are seventeen rocky islands that they say are "just off the coast of Ecuador." They're five hundred sixty three miles away. It's like saying Pigeon Forge, Tennessee is just off the coast of Manhattan.   The islands are a perfect nature preserve because there's absolutely nothing you can do with them. But the government does a great job protecting it from invading species: Your luggage is searched three times before you can get in. I got a full body search and was detained because they found an orange in my luggage; the lady behind me whizzed through customs carrying five pounds of cannabis gummies.

One of the biggest attractions is the diversity of boobies, but these birds are not as diverse as say, strip club boobies. You'll see the blue-footed booby, and then, an eight-hour cruise away, you'll see red-footed boobies . The boobies have an elaborate mating ritual that goes on all day long: The male must build a little home made of stones, painstakingly acquired one by one. Then he has to do a little dance, which the female judges harshly, like some feathered Simon Cowell. If she's not impressed, the poor booby dude has to build another whole house and get some new choreography. It seems brutal, but how many dating profiles demand: "Must have own home and love to dance."

If you want to see mating, and lots of it, check out the Galapagos sea turtles. These guys are always screwing. It's yet another thing they beat the hare at. If you go out in a dinghy, they'll hump the dinghy. (Notice, I refrained from doing a dinghy joke.) And like everything else turtles do, they mate SLOW AND STEADY. And they grunt and moan loud the whole time, like Barry White. Barry White – dead twenty-plus years and I'm still using him as a punchline. What is wrong with me?

The main activity in the Galapagos is snorkeling, and it's some of the best in the world. It feels athletic but it's just floating and watching underwater TV. And sealife is lazy, too – you see a lot of fish laying around on the bottom of the ocean, not doing anything.

I was really communing with these slackers of the deep when my tour guide swam up. He gestured to a small underwater cave. "Stick your head in there!"

I did.

"See? There's six sharks inside."

Jesus Christ! Still, I had a great story to tell. But with snorkeling, everyone always saw something better.

ME: I just stuck my head in a cave full of sharks!

BORED GUY: Yeah, we saw that. Did you see the giant squid eating a rusty shopping cart?

MY WIFE: Oh sure. I also saw an old captain with his pegleg stuck in a whale's blowhole.

ME: Goddammit.

My favorite comment on snorkeling was from Paul Reiser, who said, "Snorkeling is just swimming with a tube. And the tube just directs the water directly into your mouth."

And Jerry Seinfeld has a funny bit on scuba diving: "The main goal of scuba diving is not to die. You're just swimming there, thinking '(SINGS) Just don't die, don't die, don't die…"

All of this begs the question: Do we need both these guys? It's like there's a mad scientist in a lab churning out vaguely handsome Jewish comedians who talk about nothing. They started with Seinfeld, made a bad copy – that was Reiser, and then Garry Shandling, then Richard Belzer. Until finally they produced Richard Lewis. That's when angry villagers stormed the castle.

Chapter 6

WHAT AM I DOING IN AFRICA?

In our last chapter, we discussed the Serengeti, but there's so much more to Africa than animals. There are great cities like Johannesburg (the locals call it Jo'burg!). I was warned by friends not to visit because of apartheid, a horrible institution that had ended twenty-two years before. I even played Sun City – it's a casino and I lost eight hundred South African rand there.

I was in Johannesburg to give a speech. I told the hotel concierge I wanted to visit the local art museum. "Can I walk there?" I asked.

"Oh no no no! That's too dangerous!"

"So I should take a cab?" I asked.

"No that's even worse!"

"So you're saying if I want to see the museum, I'd have to be born there?"

He replied, "That would be best."

Johannesburg is a dangerous place. So dangerous they are actually competitive with neighboring Capetown over who has worse crime. I'd give the edge to Johannesburg, because they did something I've never seen another city do: they abandoned their downtown. I don't mean they let it slide it into ruin – they just bailed on it. The Central Business District was several square blocks of gleaming skyscrapers. It got too dangerous to work in, so one night they packed up and left. Local businesses moved to the suburbs, setting up a new downtown there. The old district is now overrun with squatters, and it's positively post-apocalyptic. There are shining high-rises with trashcan fires on the roof and laundry hanging out of every tinted-glass window.

It seemed very dangerous, but I wasn't worried. I saw smartly uniformed tourist police everywhere – they were helping visitors with luggage and inspecting tour buses. Later I learned there's no such thing as Tourist Police. These were criminals. Well-dressed criminals.

There are fifty-four countries in Africa. Let's visit ten of them…

The Wild, Wild West Africa

Arthur was skinny, middle-aged, pasty, and hairless. He looked like the Pillsbury Doughboy after gastric bypass surgery. His new wife Shasta was a gorgeous African woman half his age. They were the kind of couple only online dating could create.

We met them at a New York party, just before Arthur quit his IT job and moved to West Africa to run his wife's chicken farm. "If you're ever in the Ivory Coast, drop in," he chuckled.

Never, EVER say this to my wife, even as a joke. Not long after, she booked us a Christmas vacation to West Africa: the Ivory Coast, Ghana, Togo, and Benin. (If someone cursed my wife, "I'll see you in Hell!" she'd be on Expedia looking for flights.) Our trip started in the Ivory Coast, a surprisingly dirty place considering it's named after two brands of soap.

When we dropped in on Arthur he didn't know who the hell we were. Still, he was excited to show us around his swampy, smelly chicken farm. "I'm going to turn all this into a boutique hotel!" he exclaimed, seeing things we could not see. "We'll serve fresh eggs, chicken, capybara…"

Capybara. The world's largest rodent.

"I'll import them from South America. They'll walk freely among the guests, but I also found some great capybara recipes online." He got his wife and giant rat recipes from the same place. We decided to abandon Arthur and head north to the Ivory Coast's one major tourist attraction: the Vatican.

Yes, the Vatican.

From 1985 to 1989, the Ivory Coast spent one hundred and seventy five million dollars to build the Basilica of Our Lady of Peace. It was supposed to be an exact replica of the Vatican but just a little smaller, out of respect to Rome. Instead, by accident, it came out just a little bigger. Oopsie. It sits in the middle of the jungle, two hundred miles from the nearest city. "Guinness World Records" calls it the largest church in the world… and nobody goes there. My wife and I had the place to ourselves, and played Pope Horny and the Naughty Nun.

The African Vatican

The four countries of West Africa are shaped like four slender fingers, and next to the pointer of Ivory Coast is the upraised middle finger of Ghana. This is truly the Angriest Place on Earth. We entered Ghana at a fishing village called St. James, populated entirely by supermen – they were huge and shirtless and more muscled than anything I've ever seen in a comic book. And they were all yelling at me for no apparent reason – I had to slip several of them five-dollar bills for my crime of existing. We stepped into the St. James gym where the only sport being practiced – no surprise here – was boxing. My wife insisted I pose for a cute photo, sparring with an eight-year-old boy. The kid proceeded to beat the crap out of me. And then I had to slip him a five.

I thought we'd be safe when we checked into our luxurious (for Ghana) hotel. But that night, I got up in the middle of dinner to use the restroom. "You can't leave!" screamed the maitresse d'. "You not pay!"

"I'm going to the bathroom," I whispered.

"Pay for meal first!"

"I'll be right back," I said. "I'm just using the restroom."

"Restroom?" she cried. "Rest in a room?"

"Toilet!" I hollered. "I'M GOING TO THE TOI-LET!" Every head in the restaurant swiveled to look at me. Americans – so rude.

I saw fistfights every single day I was in Ghana. Once, my taxi driver leapt out of the car to beat up a traffic cop; then he climbed back into the cab like nothing happened. Indeed, traffic may be a big part of everyone's anger – stoplights literally take five minutes to change, and even when they do, no one can move. The traffic lights are ornamental. A new brand of commerce has developed around this traffic, as vendors weave among the stopped cars. It's not just soda, ice cream, and snacks – there are people selling shirts, shoes, and bathroom scales. One guy even had a pile of end tables stacked on his head. Plus, there are jugglers, acrobats, and fire-eaters at every intersection. It's just like Amazon Prime, only the delivery is faster and the shows are better.

Ghana does have brick-and-mortar stores, and they put a lot of thought (and paint) into the names: My God is Able Plumbing Works, Blood of Jesus Electrical, I Am the Light and the Redeemer Stationery, and the vaguely troubling In God We Trust Fast Food. It's easy to mock these, but what's so great about boring names like Lowe's Hardware or Discount Shoe Warehouse? Let's not forget, we're the home of Krispy Kreme Donuts - every word is misspelled. And their donuts are neither krispy nor kremey.

Ghana's greatest commercial product is their quirky, adorable, candy-colored coffins. According to legend, a local chieftain ordered a wooden throne built in the shape of a lion. Sadly, he died before the throne arrived (it was probably stuck in traffic), so his tribe buried him in it. Though started by accident, Ghana now has a thriving business in fantasy coffins. They can be shaped like a sports car, a six-pack of beer, a pack of Marlboros, a Ghana Airways plane – presumably whatever killed you. I thought about buying a coffin shaped like an angry maitresse d'. But somehow I'd beaten the odds, and managed to finish the week in Ghana without being murdered.

Coffin shaped like James Dean's death car.

I headed off to Togo, a much more welcoming country. They clearly see very few Caucasians because everyone greeted me warmly: "Hey White Man!" and occasionally, "Bonjour, Monsieur Leblanc!" Giggling children would run up to me and run a finger along my arm, convinced I was a black guy painted white. Babies would look at me and burst into tears, wondering, "Jesus, what happened to you?" I loved it.

I was walking down a city street when a local man whispered to me, "Psst! Wanna see a nice orphanage?" This was the same technique used to lure me into Vegas strip clubs, and in both cases it worked. I entered to see sweet African orphans making handicrafts for sale. The man clapped his hands and the children assembled onstage and sang a sweet hymn in French. "Ordinarily, they would sing more, but they have to go home now."

"They don't live here?" I asked.

"No, their parents will be picking them up soon."

"Parents?" I said. "They don't really seem to be orphans. And this doesn't seem to be much of an orphanage."

"Monsieur, it is a very fine orphanage!" He handed me a donation form. "And it is supported by generous Christians like yourself."

I guess they hadn't seen many Jews before, either.

My wife and I visited a couple of charity schools in West Africa, and they were scams, too. Each had a model classroom they'd show to American donors. In one, the date on the blackboard was from two months earlier; the lesson for the day was the too-perfect "Democracy Good – Dictatorship Evil." The room was dusty, cobwebbed, and one hundred percent kid-free. "We have three other classrooms," boasted the principal.

"Can we see them?" my wife asked.

"No!" he snapped.

Denise dashed off and peered into the three padlocked classrooms: One was full of lumber, one contained bags of cement, and the third housed an old tractor.

"I don't know how that got in there," said the principal.

We'd been in Togo; now it was time to go to Benin.

(Read that line again – the wordplay is delicious.)

We'd *been in* Togo; now it was time *to go* to Benin.

(Okay, maybe it wasn't that good.)

Before we could enter Benin, I had to get a visa from The Most Imperious Man in Africa. He had a tiny office in a run-down strip mall, but he presided over it like a potentate. He wore leopard-print pajamas and lounged on a sofa exploding with stuffing and springs. "Sit down," he commanded, yelling over an electric fan that provided lots of noise but no cooling whatsoever. I took a seat on an office chair that canted dangerously to one side.

"Did I ask you to sit there?" he said. "I did not."

I moved over to an even more busted chair. "I'd just need you to stamp our —"

"Did I ask you to speak?" he purred. "I did not."

Why not get buried in a giant pickle?

This powerless power trip lasted six hours, including his three-hour lunch break, but we were finally going to Benin. I was a man with a mission: This was the birthplace of voodoo, and I had an important question. I met with a revered witch doctor – he had a scraggly white beard, and was naked, save for a loincloth, beads, and body paint. I sat on the dirt floor of his hut and said, "I have a play opening in September. Will it be a success?"

He began a twenty-minute ritual, chanting, humming, tossing bones, burning leaves. Finally, after a long silence, he said, "No."

And you know what? He was right.

African witch doctor/theater critic.

Live and Let Libya

My wife woke me up with horrible news. "Good news! We can visit Libya now!"

It was 2006. Libya was ruled by a crazed dictator, Muammar Qaddafi. He lived in a bulletproof tent, surrounded himself with virgin female bodyguards, had a morbid fear of elevators, and always traveled with a voluptuous nurse. He wasn't even a Bond villain. He was an Austin Powers villain.

He was also a leading sponsor of world terrorism from Israel to Northern Ireland. America didn't like Libya, and, after we bombed them in '86, they weren't crazy about us. And yet somehow, suddenly, we were all friends, so my wife booked us a ten-day tour. We could monitor the delicate dance of US-Libyan relations through our visas: They were issued, withdrawn, re-issued, and – in one three-hour period – cancelled and re-re-issued. Finally, we got word that the trip was on. We'd spend Christmas in Libya, which is a very bad title for a Bing Crosby song.

I arrived on a cold December morning. My luggage did not. Our guide and our driver didn't show up either. We took a cab to our hotel in Tripoli where they informed us the power would be out for the next two days. As we lay in our dark, freezing hotel room, I said to my wife for the first time, but noooo – not the last: "You wanted to come here."

When our tour guide arrived, I was delighted to see he was obese. Here's a Traveler's Tip: You always want to have a fat tour guide, because they choose the meals. With this guy, it was a ten-day, non-stop banquet. And every meal, including breakfast, featured fresh-baked bread, rice, and French fries. It was carb-tastic. It was starch-tacular.

The guide's name was Abdul – really. And he sported a black beard and white robes. He was a walking cliché right up to the moment he opened his mouth: "Hello, my precious sweeties. I know you, I know you, I know you-ou-ou!"

Abdul was gay.

But he was born in a country, in a culture, and in a religion that condemned it. Oddly, this is a nation where male friends walk down the street holding hands, but my wife and I were told not to.

Abdul chose the tour guide life, forever on the road, delaying an arranged marriage his parents had set up. We encountered the same situation with our guide in Myanmar. He said, "I have a fiancée back home. My parents chose her. She is very ugly."

I once asked a tour guide in Honduras, "How many men in your business are gay?" He replied, "All of them but me."

Abdul was delighted my luggage was lost. He rubbed his hands together and said, "Let's go shopping!" He took me to a bus station parking lot, where I bought the beautiful three-dollar sweater I wear to this day. In the Persian bazaar, I got six pairs of fake Calvin Klein underwear for two bucks. I wore them for years in America, secretly knowing that my underpants were an enemy of the state.

My father thought we were crazy to come here; my mother was worried sick. After all, I'm not just an American – I'm a Jew. And I look really Jewish. I put myself through college modeling for hate literature. Mel Gibson paid for my senior year.

Well, guess what? The Libyans look really Jewish, too. Or maybe I look Libyan. All I know is three-quarters of the people I met there would start chatting with me in Arabic. The other quarter spoke to me in Italian. We all look alike.

This included Qaddafi – he looked just like my uncle Lou, who runs a fish market. Qaddafi's face gazed down at us from every billboard in the country. He was also or T-shirts, key rings, and bumper stickers. I even saw the man himself – he drove right past me, waving happily to crowds from his motorcade. Or maybe it was Uncle Lou from the fish market.

Qaddafi watched over us in another way: A State Security Guard accompanied our tour guide at all times, insuring that we only heard the official version of life in Libya. One day, Abdul told us the horrific story of his brother being imprisoned for four years without a trial. He then pointed to the security officer, and added with a chuckle, "If that fellow understood English, he'd hang me upside down and put a bullet in my head."

Maybe it was a joke, maybe it wasn't. To us, the security guard was a pleasant young man who insisted on carrying our luggage everywhere. It led to the oddest debate I ever had with my wife: How much do you tip the government goon?

The affable secret policeman was just one of the many paradoxes we encountered in Libya. For example, there's not a drop of alcohol to be found in the country, but the people are happily smoking themselves to death. Muslim law forbids booze, but other countries get around it. Iran has a busy bootlegging trade – they will bring top-shelf hooch right to your door. And in Saudi Arabia, supermarkets stock grape juice right next to yeast right next to sugar – all the ingredients for homemade wine.

We were a small tour group – no surprise there – but it included a retired archeology professor. I hated this guy – if it wasn't about archeology, he wasn't interested. And he assumed nobody else was, either.

ABDUL: Today we visit an Arab spice market.

PROFESSOR: Oh, I don't think anyone's interested in that.

ABDUL: Tonight we eat barbecued lamb with a Bedouin tribe.

PROFESSOR: Oh, I don't think anyone's interested in that.

ABDUL: After that, we will hear Libyan folksingers.

PROFESSOR: Oh, I don't think anyone's interested--

Actually, I agreed with him on that one.

We did spend Christmas in Libya, my first in a Muslim country. It was bizarre, because it was just another day. There was no caroling, no presents, no decorations. There was also no last-minute shopping, no family fights, no fruitcake. It was the best Christmas ever – no Christmas at all.

The tour made a stop in Benghazi, the town that launched a thousand GOP investigations. This was not a hotbed of terrorist intrigue. It was a pleasant, modern suburb, as threatening as Westchester.

But the highlight of the trip was a visit to Leptus Magna. It's an ancient Roman city whose impressive name translates to Big Bunny. For millennia, Arab invaders ignored it – they preferred nomadic tent life to big cities of stone. As a result, Leptus Magna is completely intact – you could stroll its broad avenues, explore its side streets, and browse the once-bustling market stalls.

The professor was in Seventh Dynasty heaven.

But he couldn't understand why none of us liked his corny professor jokes. He never realized that his students only laughed because he had the power to grade them. We were taking this trip pass/fail.

"That's an ionic column so keep your eye on it."

SFX: CRICKETS

What a Doric.

"My shoe size is the same as Libya's capital: Triple E."

SFX: CRICKETS

Poor guy. No one has bombed this bad in Libya since the US Air Force.

SFX: CRICKETS

Hey!

On the final day of the trip, we returned to the airport. There, I was finally reunited with my luggage. Officials had ransacked it pretty well. Two hundred and fifty dollars was missing. The government also seized my iPod so I hope Qaddafi liked Maroon 5 and "Weird Al" Yankovic.

A week after we got home, our travel agent informed us that the US had once again broken off relations with Libya – we were the last Americans allowed into the country. Tourist travel has been shut down since 2014. My wife found the one small window when it was safe to visit, and I'm glad she did.

"Carpe diem," said my Uncle Lou from the fish market. "Seize the carp."

North Africa!

Here's a sentence you won't read anywhere else in this book: My wife and I took a trip and it was my idea. I wanted to see Morocco. Why? Because it looked cool at Epcot Center.

To most kids, Epcot Center is the spinach of theme parks. Even its name, Epcot, is an acronym for Educational Park Children Only Tolerate. But I love the place. They duplicate small sections of big countries – China, Germany, France – and they do it very, very well. But my favorite place was Disney's Morocco, and I wanted to see the real thing.

And Morocco really is the real thing. It's a land of intrigue and romance right out of the movie "Casablanca" – except for the city of Casablanca. That's an ugly manufacturing port – one travel writer called it "The Cleveland of Morocco." But the rest of the country is straight from the Arabian Nights. You'll see sand dunes, blind beggars, snake charmers, and rug merchants. So many rug merchants. You walk into their showroom, they pour you a cup of tea, and then show you every carpet ever made: "You don't like this? Try this. How about this? This will look great in your home."

"You've never seen my home," I say, but it's too late.

"How is this? You like this? You buy this, I give you this…"

Once you pick a carpet, and you will pick a carpet if you want to get out of there – the negotiations begin. He will start at some exorbitant amount, say twelve zillion dollars, then immediately come down to five grand. You're excited – you've already got a bargain. You haggle back and forth, and eventually get the price down to eighteen hundred dollars. You walk out feeling like a master negotiator. Until you check Amazon and see that the most you can spend for a Persian carpet is three hundred bucks. And the one you just bought cost eighty-eight dollars.

These are real numbers, by the way. Check it out. This is why the French term for rug merchant – "marchand de tapis" – is a synonym for crook.

None of this is a putdown, by the way. The carpets are beautiful and the pitch is a piece of theater, centuries old. You are matching wits with the greatest salesmen on earth. I tried to stump one, saying: "I don't need carpets. My home has no floors."

He paused a moment, then said, "You can hang them on your walls."

Moroccans can sell anything. When I was in the city of Fez, a guy on a street corner sold me a fez. I wore the thing for awhile till I noticed nobody in Fez wears a fez. This city in Morocco was named after the Turkish city of Fez, and it's Turks who wear fezzes. As do Shriners, organ grinder monkeys, and now me.

By the way, on an absolutely ludicrous tangent, the turkey you eat at Thanksgiving is named for the country of Turkey, even though they don't come from there. There's a bird called the guinea fowl which was imported to England through North Africa. So, the English called the guinea fowl a turkey chicken even though it wasn't from Turkey and wasn't a chicken. And when British colonists first saw real turkeys in North America, they called them Turkey chickens, thinking they were guinea fowl. To sum up, our turkeys are not guinea fowl, not chickens and not even remotely from Turkey. STILL… one day, while I was walking in a suburban neighborhood in Turkey, I saw an actual turkey walking around. Just one – nobody seemed to own him. He may have been a tourist. Or maybe he was like that Fez dealer in Fez. He figured, "People expect to see a turkey in Turkey, so here I am! Gobble, gobble."

Speaking of things that don't belong there, there's a gorgeous German city plunked down in the middle of Morocco. We took a tour bus through the winding, snow-covered roads of their Atlas Mountains. We stopped at a Berber village, where locals invited us into their Berber yurt, and a carsick tourist threw up on their Berber carpeting. We continued deeper into the Moroccan mountains till we reached… Germany. At least, it looked exactly like Germany, with ski chalets, wursthauses, and biergardens. This was Ifrane, a mountain town built by German colonists homesick for the Alps. You'll find these postcard-perfect German towns popping up all over the world, including Windhoek in the Kalahari Desert of Namibia. There's another one in Brazil called Petropolis. Yes, it's a German village with a Greek name founded by a Portuguese emperor in Brazil.

Anyway… if you want the most authentic Moroccan city in Morocco, you have to visit Marrakesh. A local man offered to show me the city for two dollars.

"You mean twenty dollars," I said.

"Two dollars."

"Not twelve? "

"Two dollars."

"One, two – two dollars?" I held up two dollar bills, as a visual aid.

"Yes, two dollars! Two dollars!"

He gave me a remarkable tour – as we plunged into the city, we seemed to be receding into the past. Asphalt streets gave way to dirt roads, baseball caps turned to turbans, cars became camels. Deep in the heart of Marrakesh, we saw a cobbler in a tent, making those pointy-toed slippers only genies wear. As he cobbled away, tapping tiny nails with a tiny hammer, he watched a tiny black-and-white TV. It was showing "The Three Stooges." Not even the good "Three Stooges" – this was those crappy "Three Stooges" cartoons from the '60s.

I loved this tour right up to the moment my guide stuck out his hand and said, "Forty dollars."

I said, "No! You said two dollars!"

He looked at me with mock astonishment. Who would offer to give an all-day tour for two dollars? "Forty dollars!"

I said, "No. You said two dollars – here's two dollars."

My guide then did something truly amazing – he hopped on the back of a passing motorbike – he didn't seem to know the driver, and the bike never slowed down. My tour guide just rode off into the desert, stranding us in the depths of Marrakesh. Just before he vanished into a dust cloud, my tour guide flipped me the bird. "Fock!" he screamed. "Fock!"

"The phrase is 'fock you,'" I replied.

From Morocco we headed east to Algeria, the largest nation in Africa. It's a Muslim country and a former French colony, so it's torn between two cultures: the hospitality of the Islamic world and the snottiness of France. And for once in human history, the French won. These colonials left behind two gifts: surliness and the baguette. Every morning, you see cranky Algerians walking around, noshing on yard-long loaves of French bread. They're cheap – the cost is subsidized by the government – so the locals eat as much as they can, and drop the rest on the ground. By noon, the streets are ankle-deep in half-baguettes. It's a vaguely surreal sight – no wonder Camus set his novels here.

And he's what brought us there. My wife had booked us a tour called "In the Footsteps of Albert Camus": We'd visit his home, his school, and the park where he found inspiration. Although I'd written many book reports on Camus, I'd never read an actual book by him. I steeped myself in his work on the flight to Algeria and it was a revelation: HE SUCKED. His books were overwrought, self-pitying, and short– no wonder high school students adored them. The only reason I wanted to walk in his footsteps was to kick him in the ass.

We also visited ruins associated with Algeria's other famous author, St. Augustine. He lived in the seventh century, so the country's cranking out great writers at the rate of one every thirteen hundred years. The next one is due in the year 3322.

Algeria's other great ruin only became a ruin recently. It's the Casbah, a dark, labyrinthine neighborhood in Algiers. It survived two world wars, but couldn't survive modern plumbing. They brought running water to these ancient buildings and it undermined them – whole city blocks have collapsed in recent years.

The Casbah became famous from a line uttered by Charles Boyer in the film "Algiers": "Come wiz me to de Casbahhh." If you've never heard of Charles Boyer, he was the inspiration for cartoon skunk Pepe le Pew. And if you've never heard of Pepe le Pew, why the hell are you reading this book? What are they teaching you in school? Math?

I am the only thing holding up the Casbah.

Right next to Algeria is a much nicer country: Tunisia! Its northern coast lies on the Mediterranean and is filled with five-star resorts at one-star prices. And it's the home of the ancient Carthaginian Empire of Hannibal the Great. There's so much history in Tunisia, we hired a local professor to show us around. And while he may be quite bright in his native tongue, in English he only knew one word: "chotch." And it wasn't even a word. Any time we passed a church he'd point like a water spaniel and say it: "chotch." Like I don't know a chotch when I see one. The country also boasts a world-class history museum where, in 2015, terrorists gunned down twenty-two tourists. You can still see bullet holes in the walls and display cases.

So let me be serious for one paragraph. These terrorists did more than kill tourists – they killed that country's tourist business, wiping out the livelihoods of half a million Tunisians. We stayed in hotels where we were the only guests, ate in restaurants with no other customers. One entire tourist town had been shut down – they had to unlock the city gates to let us in. We spent a magical evening in a Tunisian cave decorated like a luxury hotel suite. That night, the owner cooked us a gourmet dinner under the stars. We were his first customers in months. It's a cliché, but when an act of violence keeps visitors away, the terrorists really do win. There's no better time to visit a place than after an attack like that. Security is extra tight, crowds are small, and the locals are so appreciative of your business. We do it all the time. You should, too.

Now… back to snark!

For a movie fan, Tunisia is a dream vacation. In the north, you can visit the Arab market where Indiana Jones shot that guy who did the thing. And in the south, you can see the locations from "Star Wars." You can walk in the footsteps Artoo Detoo. Did he have feet?

I love, love, love "Star Wars." Except for the last eight movies. And that Christmas special – what was that? But the early films were great, and their sets are still standing in the Tunisian desert. They're beautifully preserved by the warm dry climate, and you're free to walk among them, climb their stairs, open their doors. And of course, there are enterprising villagers who will rent you "Star Wars" costumes and plastic lightsabers. Best of all, when you leave town you can pick through a trash heap of authentic busted "Star Wars" props. Now you know where I do my Christmas shopping.

Here's where they shot that funny scene where Indiana Jones murdered a guy.

We find the Lost Ark... in Ethiopia?

have a friend who's a real pig. And whenever I get back from an exotic trip, his first question is, "How were the women?"

In Syria: "How were the women?"

At Chernobyl: "How were the women?"

At Arlington National Cemetery: "How were the women?"

Putting aside physical beauty, there are certain countries where women present themselves much, much better than the men. In places like Albania, Romania, and for that matter Pennsylvania, you'll see fat dudes in T-shirts and jeans accompanying women dressed like they're going to the Golden Globes. But they're not going to the Golden Globes – they're not even going to the People's Choice Awards. These women in Eastern Europe will do their hair, full make-up, put on dresses and high heels, just to sweep the sidewalk or hang wet laundry. These are poor countries where there's not money for a nice home or a decent car, but just enough disposable income to doll up one member of the couple.

Things get even stranger in Pakistan, where much of American and European apparel are made. Clothes are so cheap there that you'll see women wearing elaborately beaded and brocaded gowns to pick olives. They do farm work in dresses you'd get married in.

None of this addresses my pig friend's question about physical attractiveness. And to make it slightly less piggish, I'll address general beauty, male and female. Despite what you've learned from Borat movies, the people of Kazakhstan are gorgeous – it's at the crossroads of Europe, Asia, and India and they got the best of all worlds. And the Swedes are just as good-looking as everyone says. Many men look Chris Hemsworth and many women look like Charlize Theron. Of course, neither of them are Swedish – he's Australian and she's South African – but they're both yummy, so let it go.

But my pick for most attractive people – men women and children - is Ethiopia.

I once blurted to an Ethiopian man, "You are the most beautiful people on earth."

And he said, "Yes, we know."

Ethiopians are tall and slim, graceful with radiant smiles. And they have high, model's cheekbones, so sharp you could cut a sandwich with them. Maybe not a club sandwich, or something on a hard roll, but anything with two slices of bread. Like a grilled cheese sandwich, maybe with a slice of onion. No tomato.

But the best sandwich I ever had… no sorry, the best feature of the Ethiopians is their huge, coal-black eyes. You see this in their religious art, where dark-skinned Jesus and his apostles sport Afros and giant puppy eyes. The churches, by the way, are one of the must-see attractions of Ethiopia – they look like the great cathedrals of Europe, but they weren't built. They were sculpted out of solid rock – doors, windows, columns, roofs – all one giant piece of stone, sitting inside the quarries they were carved from. I attended a church service where they kept sacred oil n an anti-freeze jug, and sprinkled holy water from a Wesson bottle. It was a truly Christian form of frugality. The Ethiopians don't just recycle, they reuse – that Evian bottle you threw away is now filled with gasoline, which they sell at roadside stands to motorcyclists.

Not far from these stone churches you can see another pretty sacred site… The Ark of the Covenant!

The actual Ark! As in "Raiders of the Lost"! The old Nazi face-melter itself. It's housed inside a modest Ethiopian Church the size of a two-car garage. Did I get to see it? No. Has the head of the Ethiopian Church seen it? No. But they claim it's been there for three thousand years, guarded by virgin monks. Ooh, virgin monks! I'm scared.

How did the Ark wind up in Ethiopia? Well, sooner or later, EVERYTHING winds up in Ethiopia. Remember how big foosball was in the '70s and '80s? It was in every bar, every arcade, every college dorm. All those beat-up old foosball tables made it to Ethiopia – they sit outdoors, lining the back roads of the country, and everybody plays them. Foosball is the national non-sport of Ethiopia.

It's also where our old clothes go to die. The merchandise that thrift shops can't sell gets shipped to Africa. You can visit the remotest villages in this country and see locals wearing Houston Astros sweatshirts and Drexel University T-shirts; I saw an old man sporting a red Century 21 blazer and no shirt. Mostly, though, they get our old, ugly Christmas sweaters. The kids run around in sweaters adorned with snowflakes in a country where it has never, ever snowed. And they're adorable.

Ethiopian children glow like angels. These are children who have nothing, who live in houses made of mud and sticks, but they're always smiling. And they run everywhere – they have absolutely nowhere to go, but they get there fast. As my tour bus left one village, local kids ran alongside it to wave goodbye. Three miles down the road, I looked out the window and saw they were still running alongside us, keeping pace with the bus.

While they look like angels, there's a little devil to them. From village to village, kids will approach you with a worn, Xeroxed sheet of paper asking for money to buy schoolbooks. This scam, and it is a scam, is so old, it reached a second level. Soon kids were handing out a sheet reading: "Earlier requests for schoolbook money were a fraud. This one is real. Here is the book I intend to buy with your contribution."

In another village it reached a THIRD level. "Children claiming to hold schoolbooks they bought with your donation were lying. They return the book after they get your money. I encourage you to write your name in MY textbook so you'll know I can never return it."

They keep adding deception and double-cross, reaching a level of complexity somewhere between the movies "Inception" and "Tenet." But it's cute, it fools no one, and it's worth the two bucks it'll cost you.

I left rural Ethiopia and headed to the nation's capital, Addis Ababa.

We checked into a very nice hotel– previous guests had included Bill and Hillary Clinton. It was a modern place with all the bells and whistles. Just no water. The water was like a grande dame of the theater and only came on when it felt like it. We were in the dining room enjoying a typical Ethiopian meal – rich beef stew served with creepy sponge-like bread – when the manager ran to our table. "The water's about to come on! Run to your rooms! Shower! Shower!"

I had the feeling he provided a similar service to Bill Clinton when he stayed there: "Hillary's coming back to the room! Whoever's in there – get her out! Quickly! Quickly!"

We dashed up four flights of stairs to our room, stripping off our clothes on the way. We jumped into the shower together, only to hear the manager say, "You're too late. You missed it."

Still, Ethiopia is a trip I'd recommend to anyone. And I know what some of you are thinking: "Isn't there a famine there?"

Well, there was. Thirty-five years ago. To put it in perspective, when Ethiopia had its famine, the top toys in America were Verbots and Wuzzles and I don't know what the fuck either of those are. It's part of our natural inclination to learn one bad thing about a country and then think it forever.

Ethiopia is prone to food shortages and droughts. But the people I met all seemed fit and healthy. There was even one fat guy. Just one, but he was Jonah Hill when-he-was-fat fat. And he walked through the streets of Addis Ababa, eating a big sub sandwich and loving his life. People were actually cheering the guy as he walked past. Famine could kiss his big fat ass.

SIDE TRIP: The Olympics! It's Like the Olympics on Steroids!

I was at the 2008 Beijing Olympics, sitting in Beijing National Stadium. Remember this building? It looks like a giant metal bird's nest. It holds eighty thousand people. Or one giant robot vulture.

It was budgeted at half a billion, but that was deemed too much. They cut the price down to three hundred million. Then, due to cost overruns it wound up costing… half a billion dollars.

It was built to last a hundred years, but since the Olympics it's only been used a handful of times: a winter carnival, a few pop concerts. It can withstand an 8.0 earthquake but not massive public disinterest.

Not far away is the aquatic center where Michael Phelps won eight gold medals in swimming. This building looks like a huge kitchen sponge that changes colors. It's like something out of a cartoon: SpongeBob eats a taintea Krabby Patty, and falls on his back, changing hue every few seconds. It symbolizes everything I love about the Olympics: It's big and colorful and pointless and goofy. Every two years, cities across the world fight for the honor of hosting an event that will bankrupt them. Not only do the Olympics lose money, they leave towns stuck with expensive facilities nobody uses, like a velodrome. If you don't know what a velodrome is, it proves my point.

The locals don't want the games – I lived in Los Angeles during the 1984 Olympics and the entire city cleared out. It was the perfect LA – lots of palm trees, no people. A spokesman for Disneyland said the park was so empty you could shoot deer in the parking lot. Weird metaphor from the studio that made Bambi.

Everyone left Los Angeles but me. So I bought the cheapest Olympic ticket I could find: a boxing match between Egypt and Cameroon. These are not big boxing countries and the two fighters had clearly never seen a fight before. One guy huddled in a corner trying not to get hurt; the other guy rocked from side to side like a man on a ship in a typhoon. I've never been in a fight in my life, but I knew I could whip both these guys at the same time.

I went to the London Olympics in 2012, and that bustling city hasn't been so empty since the blitz. Still, I couldn't get tickets to the Opening Ceremony – the one that featured those lovable geezers Paul McCartney, Eric Idle, and Queen Elizabeth. So I watched the ceremony in a hotel suite, surrounded by former Olympic athletes. They couldn't get tickets either. Because, if you don't win a medal, you don't get squat. And each year six thousand Olympic competitors go home empty-handed.

On TV, I watched Sebastian Coe open the Games – Coe won four Olympic medals for running real far, real fast. For that, he was elected to Parliament and was made a Lord; tonight he was addressing a TV audience of 3.5 billion – half the people on earth.

Sitting next to me in that dingy hotel room was the runner Sebastian Coe beat by two seconds. He's now a gym teacher in Connecticut.

Even if you win, that's no guarantee of anything. Sure, George Foreman, Muhammud Ali, and Joe Frazier went from the Olympics to long, lucrative careers beating each other up. Mary Lou Retton morphed from Olympic gymnast to a beloved Peter Pan on stage. General George S. Patton competed in the 1912 Olympics in pistol shooting; he came in twenty-first. Patton would go on to become the least beloved Peter Pan in history.

And what about Primos Kozmus? No, he's not the bad guy in the Transformers movies, but that's an excellent guess. Primos Kozmus is the guy I saw that night in Beijing's Bird's Nest Stadium – he won Slovenia's first medal in the hammer throw. He spent his whole life – ignoring his studies, sacrificing his personal life – to become the world's greatest hammer throwerer-er. Now that he won the gold medal, what could he do? Work at Home Depot, throwing hammers from the stockroom to the front of the store?

Why had I even seen the hammer throw? Because tickets were ten bucks. It costs a fortune to see Pairs Figure Skating at the Winter Olympics; but it's easy to get into Pairs Figure Skating Rehearsal. You see the same skaters, the same routines, but many numbers end with the couples screaming at each other. On the ice. In front of everyone. And that's what I go to the Olympics for.

You see, I'm not really a sports fan. As a result, I attend the events no one else is interested in: trampoline; race walking; roller hockey. I'm only sad that I missed these actual Olympic Sports that were tried out and retired: hot air ballooning; club swinging; live pigeon shooting. Everyone remembers Jesse Owens' victories in the 1936 Olympics; but no one recalls Charles Downing Lay, who also won the gold medal for America that year in… Town Planning. Town Planning was an Olympic event!

No matter how obscure the sport, you get caught up in it – within ten minutes, you consider yourself an expert. "Nice step rhythm!" I heckled the javelin thrower. "You throw like women's javelin world record holder Barbora Sportakova!"

My wife jostled me. "Maybe you shouldn't antagonize the man with the pointy stick and the deadly aim."

Yes, I embody another fundamental aspect of the Olympics: bad sportsmanship. A Russian athlete told me, "I only want English or American referees – they are the only honest judges. Even better is a Russian referee, because they cheat, but for me." Politics ruins every Olympics just like it ruins every family's Thanksgiving dinner.

Still, the Games take me all over the globe, and they're generally a reflection of the city hosting them. The 1984 LA Olympics were a showbizzy affair: They opened with a speech by movie star-turned-president Ronald Reagan. They closed with the arrival of a fake UFO dubbed "the flying taco."

At the other end of the spectrum was Pyongchang, South Korea, the tiny onion-growing town that hosted the Winter Games.

I asked a local taxi driver to take me to the Olympic Park.

He gave me a blank stare.

I said, "It's the Olympics! It's the only thing in this town!"

Blank stare.

I showed him a brochure for the Olympics. It had a map. Olympic Park was written in Korean. Still, none of this got through to him.

I exploded. "It's two miles away! It's that big complex of sports arenas rising from the onion fields! It has a blimp floating over it! I'm pointing right at it! Follow my finger!"

I wound up walking to the Olympics. It was two miles in freezing weather and high winds; when I arrived, I found out all my events had been canceled due to freezing weather and high winds. They promised me a full refund. It's been six years and I'm still waiting.

That night, after the games I didn't see, I had to get home. I found another cabbie, and gave him a card with the name and address of my hotel. He looked it over, seemed to consider it a gift, and pocketed it. And then the blank stare.

"It's at the beach!" I said. I mime ocean waves, surfing, swimming, a shark. He seemed to enjoy my little show, which was nice, but I was not getting through to him. "It's at the ocean! The Pacific Ocean! How can you not know where it is? It is literally – LITERALLY – the largest thing on earth!"

Still, Pyeongchang was more prepared than Athens. They were hosting the 2004 Olympics, and I was in town a few months before. I visited the site of their Olympic Park and saw nothing. Just acres and acres of mud. There were actually more facilities at the ruins of the original Greek Olympics built twenty-seven hundred years before.   The 2004 Athens Olympics were budgeted at five billion, cost eleven billion, and may be the reason Greece is still in debt today.

The best-run games I ever attended were the 2014 Sochi Winter Olympics. If you remember them at all, it was for the negative coverage they got in American media: Sochi was a tropical resort, all the snow was melting, and the town was overrun with stray dogs. What a load of borscht – Sochi was plenty cold, much cooler than the seventy-degree weather at Vancouver's Winter Olympics. And I only saw two stray dogs in the weeks I spent there. Security seemed tight – there were metal detectors everywhere, but not one of them was plugged in.

It was a new Russia –the people were cheerful, helpful, and friendly. Clearly, the order had been given to be nice to tourists, because the moment the Olympics ended, the Russians went back to being surly, sad, and drunk.

I attended the Opening Ceremony, sitting directly across the arena from Vladimir Putin. As the magnificent spectacle unfurled, I watched Putin – what was he thinking? Was he proud? Relieved? Bored?

It turns out, what he was thinking was, "In three weeks, I'm invading the Ukraine."

Chapter 7

WHAT AM I DOING IN ASIA?

A

sia is the biggest landmass on earth, and it has something for everyone.

Ho Chi Minh City is the fastest-moving city – it left me a nervous wreck and I live in Times Square New York. The streets of this Vietnamese city are choked with motorbikes moving at breakneck speed – some carry a family of five, others carry a bushel of hay or a dozen squawking geese in cages. If you need to get across the street… well, you can't. Give it up. Make other plans. Make a life on this side of the road.   By the way, Saigon formally changed its name to Ho Chi Minh City thirty-five years ago. Everyone who lives there still calls it Saigon.

After a stressful trip to Ho Chi Minh City, I recommend Laos. You may know it as that country we bombed the crap out of for no apparent reason. We dropped as many bombs on this tiny country during the Vietnam War as we did on all of Europe AND Asia during World War II. There are bars and restaurants in Laos decorated with unexploded munitions. And you thought eating at Chipotle was risky…

Although we dropped nearly a ton of bombs for every person in Laos, it's the most laid-back country on earth. If you walk into any shop, there's a good chance the owner is behind the counter, laying in a hammock, sleeping like a baby. I was always torn: Should I wake him up to make a purchase, or let him snooze? Generally, I'd take what I needed, leave money on the counter, and tiptoe out. A major recreation in Laos is inner tubing on a river, a sport so mellow, you could win a race in a coma. This was the true Prozac Nation.

There was only one stressed-out person in the country: our tour guide. His name was Bam, but for some reason my wife kept calling him Boo. One day he brought us to breakfast and told us he would pay for it. My wife asked, "What can we order?"

"Anything you want," said Bam.

"Thank you, Boo," said my wife.

After Bam left, my wife proceeded to order three omelets, fruit, sausage, bacon, ham, coffee, decaf, and dry wheat toast. I ordered scrambled eggs.

"That's all? Boo said you could have anything."

"I think he meant any one thing on the menu, not every single thing in Laos."

She replied, "Well, one of us is right, and one of us is wrong."

Well, for the only time I can recall in our marriage, I was right. When our tour guide came back and saw the bill for breakfast, he exploded. Bam went boom. He screamed, he turned purple, and I swear I saw steam shoot out of his ears. Finally, I told him, "Don't worry, Bam. I'll pay the bill."

It was only eight bucks. Nice country.

Malaysia is another nice country with no particular reason to visit it. We were lured there by their firefly tourism: You sail down a river at night and see maybe fifty fireflies. That's more than I can see in Manhattan. It's about what I could see in Brooklyn. It's a lot less than I'd see in Queens. Still, it got me there. Now what? Well, Malaysia threw up a bunch of little museums to entertain tourists: a glass museum, a gold museum, a ghost museum, a glow-in-the-dark museum; there are museums dedicated to toys, tech, and tunnels; there's an Owl Museum and the Meowseum of Cat Art. And those are just in one city: Penang.

Literally the biggest attraction in Malaysia is the Petronas Towers, a double skyscraper in Kuala Lumpur. The Petronas Towers are like the Winklevoss Twins: They're huge, there's two of them, and they were impressive fifteen years ago. Up to 2004, the Petronas Towers were the tallest buildings in the world. Now they're tied for seventeenth place.

Malaysia is a crossroads for world cuisine. The food is wonderful and a common greeting is, "What did you eat today?" Nonetheless, they seem most obsessed with their durians. Huge swaths of the country are devoted to growing these so-called fruits. They are lopsided bowling balls covered with sharp spikes, and they stink like rotten meat – there are signs in every hotel saying "No Durians." And every salesman makes the same joke: "Tastes like heaven, stinks like hell." And I agree, except for the "taste like heaven" part. They use durians in cookies, shakes, candy, and cakes and it's all like biting into a fart. They offend nearly every sense: taste, smell, vision, touch. Everything about them urges you not to eat them. The Japanese can't get enough.

DURIANS!

Woo-Hoo! Wuhan!

Except for launching the plague that sickened millions and cratered the world economy, Wuhan is a pretty nice place. With a population of eight and a half million, it's what the Chinese consider "a small town." I was there a few years back as part of a junket, teaching Chinese filmmakers about my work on "The Simpsons," a show they neither watched nor heard of. The lone fan I met had me autograph a Chinese box set of "Simpsons" DVDs that was handsomely packaged and entirely fake. But pretty much everything you buy in China is fake: purses, perfume, pork products. "You cannot trust the Chinese," said my Chinese guide, an intense little woman named Yao. "They will screw you over. Big time!"

Yao had conceived and organized this whole trip. Midway through our twelve-hour flight from LA to Beijing, she cautioned me that unscrupulous Chinese producers would want to make deals with me. "I will protect you," she said.

"Thank you."

"I want five percent!" She immediately pulled a contract from her (fake) Louis Vuitton handbag. I signed the document, fearing that if I didn't, she would push me off the plane at thirty thousand feet. I hadn't even landed in China and I'd already been extorted. Yao didn't seem happy either. As the jet touched down in Beijing, she told me, "Five percent is too low. I want ten!"

"No! I already signed a contract. Your contract!"

She moaned. Yao had even screwed over Yao.

Our first stop in Beijing was with the Chinese Minister of Animation. "I regulate every cartoon produced in China and report on each studio to the government," explained this unsmiling man in an old-school woolen Mao jacket. "I am also the voice of Chinese Donald Duck."

The Minister showed me his newest project: Peking Opera stories adapted to cartoon form. He hoped these would get teenagers interested in this ancient Chinese art. He showed me one five-minute cartoon, and asked my opinion. "You must be honest," he said, taking a grim pull from a coffee mug emblazoned with a grinning Donald Duck.

"Honestly?" I said. "I found it really boring and couldn't imagine a teenager enjoying it."

"I see," he grunted. "We have made one hundred and forty of those."

And this is the problem: the Chinese have the fastest-growing movie business in the world, producing films that gross billions domestically and zilch overseas. Chalk it up to cultural differences: Foreigners don't like bad movies. And they are bad – ponderous historical dramas, sexless romances, and comedies so screechy and pointless, not even the French enjoy them.

From Beijing, we moved on to Harbin, Hubei, Guangzhou, Guangdong, Gangplow, and Guanaco. They're all cities larger than New York, and I'd never heard of any of them – have you? If so, you're lying – Gangplow is a farming tool and Guanaco is a kind of llama. All these cities are built on the basic Chinese model – plow under three millennia of history and replace it with gleaming clusters of skyscrapers, shopping malls, KFC, and knock-offs of KFC (KLC, KLG, UFO, and yes, OFC – Obama Fried Chicken).

My favorite city was Guangdong – called Canton when we were kids, it was rechristened Guangdong in the dumbest name change since Kanye West became Yeezy. The city is filled with the kind of weird wonders you'd only see in China:

– The parks are packed with old people playing hacky-sack (actually, a local variant, featuring a dart on a spring). They seniors play it all day long and have gotten really good at it. Why do they do it? The government told them to, to keep them busy. And they'll keep at it till the government gives them permission to stop. Or die.

– The entire skyline – two dozen buildings – have been covered with LEDs, and every night, the city becomes one big video screen. This being China, they have all the technology and no idea what to do with it – the night I was there, the presentation was ten minutes of giant goldfish swimming from building to building. They'd turned the whole city into a screensaver.

– They built a long glass observation deck protruding over a thousand-foot-deep gorge. To make this even scarier, it's brooded over by a giant concrete sculpture of King Kong. Or rather, a rip-off of King Kong – it wouldn't be a Chinese attraction without some copyright infringement.

While in Guangdong, I visited the animation studio that produced Bunko, "the Bart Simpson of China." And their Bart looked a lot like our Bart – spiky hair, blue shorts, yellow skin. The only difference was Bunko was twice as tall. And had no nose. I met Bunko's creator, a handsome young man called "the Matt Groening of China" who had a much bigger, nicer office than Matt Groening, "the Matt Groening of America." Bunko's bunker was a six-story animation complex, with state-of-the-art studios, art gallery, and gift shop. What they didn't have was viewers. Though they assured me

Bunko was a world-wide phenomenon, no one I met in China had ever heard of it. Animation fans have never heard of it. Google has never heard of it. The whole gorgeous studio may have been a front for a meth lab or a money-laundering operation. Maybe that's why they called it Bunko.

Nothing much had come of this junket until I met Dr. Fu (not his real monosyllable), "the Walt Disney of China." By now you may have noticed that everything in their country is "the [BLANK] of China." Their top attraction should be called "'The Great Wall of China' of China."

Dr. Fu owns China's largest amusement park; he also runs the best aquarium I've ever visited and the only entertaining circus I've ever seen. (Screw you, Cirque Du Soleil.) And he owns a zoo packed to the rafters with exotic animals. Think rhinos are an endangered species? Not at Fu Zoo, where you see way too many rhinos, all packed into one enclosure. Excited to see one panda cub? This zoo has the world's only set of panda triplets, in clear violation of China's one child policy.

Are they really triplets? All panda cubs look alike, so it's possible they grabbed three cubs from three mothers and put them in one pen. Or that they pumped one poor panda mom full of fertility drugs. Or they fattened up and repainted some beagle puppies. My theory is that Dr. Fu put a gun to a female panda's head and hissed in her ear, "Have triplets." Dr. Fu is a very intimidating character, so much so that I'm going to call him Dr. Wo for the rest of this article. Even his alias needs an alias.

Wo gets what Wo wants, and on this visit Wo wanted me. He invited me to his private dining room, where, in true Bond villain fashion, one entire wall was a fish tank full of great white sharks. "I want you to make an animated film about my panda triplets. And fifty-two episodes of a panda cartoon series," he told me. "How long will that take?"

It would probably take four years, but knowing he wouldn't have the patience for that, I told him two years.

"I want it in six months," he said.

"You got it!" I told him. It was a physically impossible task, but no one says no to Wo. As his assistant lamented to me, "He once ordered me to get him a whale. Where do you buy a whale?"

My tour guide Yao emailed me that night, warning me to be careful dealing with Dr. Wo. "I know," I wrote back, "he's a slippery character."

And, for reasons I'll never figure out, Yao forwarded my email to Dr. Wo. The man had just made me a hugely generous offer and I called him a slippery character. Wo canceled our deal, and Yao and I returned to America empty-handed.

Why did she do it? This could be a million-dollar deal. With the five percent commission she extorted from me, Yao stood to clear a cool fifty thousand dollars. It's like she knew that in a Chinese deal, someone had to get screwed – even if it meant double-crossing her own client, and as a result, her triple-crossing herself.

Since that visit to China, Yao and I haven't spoken. One of the local mayors I met has gone to jail. Dr. Wo has been accused of flying helicopters at night into Africa to kidnap giraffes. No one has ever seen a Bunko cartoon. And I learned that every night at midnight in Times Square, all the buildings light up in an elaborate video show even better than the one in Guangzhou.

It's just three blocks from my apartment. But who wants to go to Times Square at midnight?

This collection of Chinese "Simpsons" DVDs is as handsome as it is fake.

The King Kong of Guangdong.

Tokyo is Okey-Dokey-o

The Chinese word for crisis is the same as the word for opportunity. Business gurus says this all the time, so naturally it's complete bullshit. The Chinese word for crisis is "crucial point of danger." Or, more simply, the Chinese word for "crisis" is… "crisis."

But for my wife Denise, the word crisis really does mean opportunity. After Japan's Fukushima disaster led to three nuclear meltdowns, my wife said, "We have to go there."

This sounded crazy, even for her. Visiting Tokyo right after a nuclear accident would be like taking a vacation in Chernobyl. Something we also did.

I asked her, "Why would we would go to Japan right after three nuclear meltdowns?"

She replied, "The lines will be shorter at Tokyo Disneyland."

Well, she sold me. I love Disneyland, and we'd been to every other one on earth. They're all like the cities that built them. Hong Kong Disneyland, like Hong Kong, amazes you with how much they can pack into a limited space. Conversely, Shanghai Disneyland, like Shanghai itself, is sprawling – too sprawling in fact. There's only a handful of rides and they're miles apart. As soon as you've gotten from the front gate to the Tron Roller Coaster, it's closing time. As for Disneyland Paris, it's just like the rest of Paris – achingly beautiful, yet filled with cigarette butts and unimpressed Frenchmen. It's the Disenchanted Kingdom; the Surliest Place on Earth. I got slammed square in the back by a car from the Snow White Ride; the attendant just laughed a French laugh: "Haw haw haw." I was mocked by a grown man dressed as Dopey.

In Morocco, we visited Disneyland Casablanca. It was just one ride – a rusted-out kiddie coaster that didn't go anywhere. Kids climbed aboard and sat there contentedly for twenty minutes. Despite the large hand-painted sign – DIZEELAND – this may not have been an authorized park.

We'd never been to Tokyo Disneyland because we'd heard it was way too crowded – a six-hour wait for any decent ride. Maybe having the worst nuclear disaster since Chernobyl would keep the crowds down.

It didn't, really. The place was packed, just not jam-packed. Full to the rafters but not bursting at the seams. You can skip Tokyo's Magic Kingdom: it's exactly like Orlando's. But there's a second park next door – DisneySea – and it's built on a titanic scale – literally: there's a full-size copy of the Titanic sitting in the middle of the park. They've duplicated nine-square blocks of Venice where you can take gondola rides. And there's a life-size volcano with a roller coaster inside it.

We left Tokyo Disney glowing with childish wonder and nuclear radiation. But how would we fill the rest of the trip? Japan is a beautiful country with a rich culture, but there's not much to see. Just think of your monster movies – when Godzilla goes on a rampage in Japan, there's no landmarks for him to destroy, no iconic buildings to climb. He's always just walking into power lines. So many power lines.

I felt like Godzilla – what was I gonna do in Japan for the next two weeks?

And my wife said the words that make my blood run cold: "Let me surprise you."

My wife and I were married on Labor Day 1988, and I figured this was the last party I'd be hosting for awhile. But FOUR DAYS LATER, I climbed out of the bathtub, walked into my living room, and heard "SURPRISE!" My wife had thrown me a surprise birthday party. While these things look cute on TV shows, it's about the worst experience you can have. One moment you're relaxed and alone; a second later, you're hosting a party you didn't even know was happening. I was wet, naked, and surrounded by scary people. It was birth all over again.

THREE DAYS AFTER THAT Denise and I were dining out when she complained that her steak was overcooked. The waiter insisted it was rare. This escalated into a shouting match, with the waiter proclaiming: "I will prove to you the steak is rare!" Out of the kitchen walked a cow – or rather two people in a ratty cow suit – who proceeded to dance around my table. My wife had surprised me again – twice in the week since our wedding. I began to fear that this is what married life would be: my wife springing giant surprises on me every few days, pranking me to an early grave. But Denise lost her taste for entertaining me – that's the beauty of marriage. She retired her surprise skills till this trip to Japan, twenty-five years later.

First, she booked us a suite at the Godzilla Hotel. Yes, Godzilla had no landmarks to destroy in Tokyo, so he became one himself. It's a four-star businessman's hotel that has a life-size Godzilla bursting through the roof. A Godzilla paw smashed through the wall of our hotel room, just above the bed. Godzilla props adorned the walls, and when you turned the TV, you saw specially made news reports about Godzilla attacking our hotel. I went to the toilet in the middle of the night: Suddenly the room went dark, the walls shook, and Godzilla appeared in the bathroom mirror. This was too goddam much Godzilla.

From there, Denise found us an even scarier hotel room: the Hello Kitty Suite. Hello Kitty adorned

the wallpaper, the curtains, the carpet. It was on the towels and slippers. Breakfast arrived and it was a Hello Kitty shaped omelet, with Hello Kitty faces burned into the toast.

It all put me in mind of an amazing news story from the eighties. A man was so obsessed with sex that he covered every square inch of his home with porn: floors, walls, ceiling, furniture – even appliances. This still wasn't enough, so he fashioned a porn helmet: a lampshade lined with dirty pictures that he wore on his head, so he could always be looking at pornography. Sadly, one day his porn helmet got hooked on his porn chandelier, and he accidentally hanged himself. Substitute porn with creepy cartoon cat and his apartment becomes the Hello Kitty Suite.

I'd be surrounded by more kitties – real-life ones – in Tokyo's many cat cafés. These are just what they sound like – intimate coffee houses with lots of cats roaming around, climbing on everyone and everything. They proved so popular that they spawned many imitators – owl cafés, snake cafés, hedgehog cafés, and even one capybara café – somehow, South America's largest rodent wound up in a Tokyo Starbucks. We have nothing like this in America except for New York's many rat and roach cafés.

We tried different theme restaurants for dinner: the Pirate Steakhouse, the Vampire Diner, the Ninja Bistro. And the thing to understand about all these places is there's nothing cheesy about them. There is full commitment to the themes – the pirate restaurant looked and smelled like an authentic sailing ship; the Vampire Diner scared the crap out of me. In Japan, there's no line between high culture and low, between entertainment for kids and for adults. If Japan had Chuck E Cheese, the pizza would actually be good and the mouse would be anatomically correct.

One day we stopped at a coffee shop done in early Sid and Marty Krofft. The walls were a psychedelic nightmare; plastic vines dripped from the ceiling. Giant fiberglass mushrooms with eyes rolled between tables bringing coffee. Japanese businessmen filled this place. One floor up was another coffee shop, but in this one the waitresses all were dressed as French maids, wearing impossibly short skirts. This joint was populated with happy families. To my mind, the Japanese never quite knew where to put their sex. I saw an insanely sexy TV commercial one morning; I thought it was for a strip club, but it was actually for Post Honeycomb cereal. Conversely, the logo of the local massage parlor was a cartoon rabbit in a bikini.

The Japanese, in fact, don't do anything the way you expect. In November they have some of the most beautiful fall colors on earth. But they don't go out to see them during the day when there's, you know, the sun. It's a nighttime thing: They floodlight the parks and temples of the city so you can enjoy the fall colors when it's dark. And cold.

They also stage a daily parade of giant illuminated robots. It's a jaw-dropping spectacle, but for some reason they do it indoors, in a cramped ballroom you couldn't hold a wedding in. Spectators are jammed against the walls, as the robots plow straight through, clearly on their way to a better event.

For fun, the Japanese play pachinko, a game which is no fun at all. It's a combination of pinball, but with no control of the ball, mixed with a slot machine that never ever pays out money. If Satan wanted an ironic punishment for people who wasted their lives playing video games, he'd have invented pachinko. Nine million players sit cheek by jowl for hours, joylessly playing this game – it looks like a scene cut from "The Matrix" for being too depressing. Pachinko generates thirty times as much money as Vegas, with ten thousand arcades as cacophonous and smoke-filled as Tom Waits.

The biggest mystery about Japan is where's all the garbage? Tokyo's a city of twelve million people, and they're all snacking on food that looks like candy and tastes like fish. They're producing tons of trash daily, but you don't see a scrap of litter anywhere. And they're not throwing it away, either, because THERE ARE NO TRASH CANS IN TOKYO. There was an attack in 1995 where terrorists planted sarin nerve gas in the city trash bins. Japan responded by banning all garbage cans. In America, we sell machine guns to mental patients; these guys have outlawed trashcans for twenty-five years. So where's all the litter? Where's the wrappers from the chewy salmon bars and the sticks from their squid popsicles? I don't know. I guess they eat those, too.

If you get lost in Tokyo, the locals are always happy to help. Unfortunately, they may be lost too – it's a big city. And if you ask someone for directions, it's considered rude to say "I don't know." Instead, they'll make something up. It won't get you where you're going, but it'll get you away from them.

We did explore the culture of Japan. We went to see kabuki theater, where actors in weird masks scream at each other for six hours. The music seemed to be twanging bedsprings and people banging on all those trashcans they'd taken off the streets. Maybe it made sense to the locals, but I didn't see one Japanese person in the audience. It was all baffled tourists. Either the Japanese see kabuki once as kids and decide "that's enough for me." Or it's just a big prank they've been pulling on tourists for a thousand years.

We also visited Tokyo's Museum of Tobacco and Salt. It's a large and beautiful institution that answers all your questions except "Why did they build this?" These aren't big Japanese products. Tobacco represents 0.2 percent of their agricultural output. As for salt – they don't produce Grain One. No salt at all! The museum seemed so random. What concepts were rejected? The Museum of Shoes and Butter? Toothpaste & Trolley Cars?

One of my favorite attractions was the Pitch-Black Pilgrimage. We found a few of these in the basements of Buddhist temples: It's one long, serpentine path you stumble through in total darkness. Tour books say it represents the path through the Buddha's mother's womb and when I emerged, I really felt reborn. But my tour guide told me the more likely story: I was a piece of food working my way through the Buddha's intestines. And suddenly, I felt like shit.

We also took an 'kebana class – the Japanese art of flower arrangement. It seems like a no-brainer – flowers are pretty to begin with. It's hard to mess them up, right? Wrong! At least according to our instructor. "Terrible. That is awful. Ugly ugly ugly." She shoved me aside and adjusted one pussy willow a fraction of an inch. "Now. Perfect."

My favorite cultural activity was an aikido class. This is Japanese martial art where an entire match can take a tenth of a second. You can see these bouts on YouTube – they're literally over in the blink of an eye. Can you imagine settling in for a night of Monday Night Aikido? You've got a six-pack of sake and a hot shrimp sundae, and suddenly the whole thing's over while you're still sinking into the couch. Still, it was fun to do. My wife and I put on protective padding. heavy woolen kimonos, and steel face masks. Then we wailed away at each other with sticks. It was a great way to get out some aggression after a stressful day of flower arrangement, and thirty-four years of marriage. It was all in good fun until somehow – SOMEHOW – my wife got through all my protective gear and smacked me square in the groin with a bamboo pole. Just another one of her little surprises.

From Russia With Like

The 23 and Me test told me I was ninety-nine point three percent Jewish, and I thought, "Really, that little?" And when you're Jewish, you don't care about revisiting your roots. Because this isn't the country you came from, it's the country you were chased out of. In my case, I'm half Russian, and my family's story is so sad it makes "Fiddler on the Roof" look like a musical. I mean, "Fiddler on the Roof" is already a musical, but I was referring to a happy musical like "Annie" not a sad one like, uh, "Fiddler on the Roof."

Nonetheless, I've visited Russia twice: the first time, with a tour group in 2001. The country was not quite ready for us. Every couple of hours our tour bus would stop in the woods and our guide would tell us, "This is your toilet stop. This is truly a wonderful forest to urinate in." It was summer, the temperatures hovered around a hundred degrees, and the hotels had no air conditioning. Each night, you could sleep with the windows open and be eaten alive by mosquitoes, or close the windows and be baked alive. Those were your options: Freedom of choice had come to Russia. Crime had come too – there was no restaurant, bar or hotel in any corner of the world's largest country that was not being shaken down by the Russian mob.

The tour group I was traveling with was largely elderly and largely never shut up. But their endless chattering stopped abruptly when we entered Red Square and laid eyes on The Kremlin. They were children of the Cold War and this building represented pure evil and the threat of nuclear annihilation. Now the red brick building with the candy-colored domes seemed cute and small and toothless – just like them.

For the record, the Kremlin is the fortified wall around Red Square. What everyone calls the Kremlin is actually St. Basil's Cathedral, not the seat of power for an atheistic Communist regime. It's like confusing the White House with the Waffle House, which was true only during the Clinton Administration.

Not far from what everyone calls the Kremlin is Lenin's Tomb, a structure no bigger than a carwash. You descend a short flight of steps to visit the waxy figure that may be Lenin, but is probably a wax figure. There are large signs in several languages reading "DO NOT MAKE JOKES." So, of course, I made a joke. I asked, "Do they dress Lenin in different outfits for the holidays?" My wife laughed and guards pointed machine guns at her.

Interestingly, the Russians want to get rid of Lenin's Tomb – it honors a man who brought the country a repressive regime that collapsed after seventy years. It's only open to make the tourists happy, as I'm sure Trump's Tomb someday will be. The sooner the better, I say.

It's Lenin's Tomb – no joke!

I went back to Russia two decades later, and everything had changed. The Cold War was over and Western decadence had won. Moscow's Tverskaya Street rivaled New York's Fifth Avenue for high-end shopping and fine dining. Good food in Russia? That's a revolution! It was a warm Russian winter, with temperatures in the high nothings, and this once-godless country had gone cuckoo for Christmas. Red Square went over the top with lights and decorations; wherever there wasn't real snow, there was fake snow. Lenin's Tomb was flush up against Santa's Workshop.

In true capitalist spirit, I was in Russia on business: I'd been asked to give a lecture on "The Simpsons" to an audience of Soviet entrepreneurs. Whenever I get an offer like this, my first question is always, "Who did you ask first?" In this case, it was Uma Thurman. Of course. If you can't get the gorgeous, world-famous actress, bring in some Jew you never heard of. But the weird surprise was they had heard of me – the Russians, for some reason, go absolutely Bolshoi for "The Simpsons"! When my limo arrived at the hotel – yes, they sent a limo! – I was mobbed by paparazzi. Autograph hounds waved publicity photos of me that I didn't even know existed. My hotel, by the way, was the Moscow Ritz, where Donald Trump allegedly romped and, let's say, "showered" with four prostitutes. Having stayed there, I believe it – my suite was so luxurious, you'd feel like you could get away with anything. And the décor was so baroque, the KGB could hide cameras anywhere.

Papparatski in Moscow.

I arrived at the venue the next morning – it was Moscow Olympic Stadium, and I'd be addressing fifteen thousand Russian entrepreneurs. That's a lot of entrepreneurs for a former Communist dictatorship. Many in the audience spoke English – the rest received simultaneous translation through headphones. The opening speaker was announced: Richard Gere! He strolled onstage to dead silence. He flashed his dazzling movie star grin and proclaimed, "Hello Moscow! I love this city!"

More dead silence.

None of the speakers who followed him got much response either – not Malcolm Gladwell, not the Ultimate Fighting Champion of the World. We were a pretty random assortment of speakers – the only thing we had in common was that nobody wanted to listen to us. It was seven hours of thunderous indifference, broken up by a lunch where the businessmen downed liquor like Prohibition was coming back. I was the final speaker, and, as BBC Russia reported, "Tonight, Mike Reiss told great jokes to a gravely silent audience."

I shrugged it off – I figured this was how Russian audiences always were. I asked the Russian organizer how she thought the day went.

She said, "This was a complete disaster. Tomorrow, they are tearing down the stadium."

That's a pretty harsh review – you were so bad, they tore down the venue. Still, I felt proud. My ancestors left this country a century ago without a penny in their pockets. I was leaving with a speaker's fee of ten thousand dollars.

When I got home, the check bounced. It bounced and bounced and may still be bouncing. I've lectured on "The Simpsons" in twenty-two countries and that's the only time that happened. You can read about it in my "Simpsons" memoir "Springfield Confidential." It's available in English, Spanish, German, and we recently sold the Russian-language rights.

That check bounced, too.

Malcolm Gladwell and I share a happy moment before bombing in Moscow.

SYNERGY
GLOBAL
FORUM

26-27 ноября, Москва, СК Олимп

МАЙК РЕЙСС

СЦЕНАРИСТ И ПРОДЮСЕР
МУЛЬТСЕРИАЛА «СИМПСОНЫ»

СИНЕРГИЯФОРУМ.Р

Now appearing in Moscow: Mank Penis!

Nepal: Over the Hills and Fart Away

My plane was flying into Lukla, better known by pilots across the globe as "The World's Most Dangerous Airport." It deserved the title – I've been to fashion shows with longer runways. "We've safely landed in Nepal," announced the captain, unable to hide his relief. "Please set your watches back forty-five minutes." Forty-five minutes? This was going to be a weird place.

The weirdness began instantly, when I visited a large Buddhist temple and met their High Lama. A wizened man in red robes and long white beard, he certainly looked the part. And then he opened his mouth. "Ah betcha wanna take mah picture," he said in a Tennessee twang. "Jes' make sure you don't steal mah soul. Hey-hey!" He dressed like the Dalai Lama but talked like Dolly Parton. Clearly, decades ago, he'd been a hippie hiking through Nepal, found God, and never left.

Nepal has been a haven for hippies, aging hippies, and recovering hippies since the sixties. And why not? The entire country is like one big commune – it's as if, after all the bands left Woodstock,

I meet the Lama of Lynchburg, the Buddha of Bourbon country.

the half-million spectators stayed behind and declared it the Sovereign Kingdom of Groovy. Also, like Woodstock, there's ankle-deep mud everywhere you go. The Nepalese people, young and old, even dress like hippies in colorful, mismatched outfits: paisley scarves, plaid shirts, day-glo knit caps, and Scooby-Doo pajama pants. Everyone looks like they got dressed in a thrift shop during a blackout.

In keeping with the hippie theme, freak flags are flying everywhere – strings of multi-colored pennants hang all over Nepal, zigzagginging through forests, across chasms, up one side of the Himalayas and down the other. While it's very beautiful, I wish they'd strung up fewer prayer flags and more power lines.

Electric power here is spotty; however, every hotel has a sign announcing FREE WI-FI. None of

Too many flags, not enough power lines.

them have wi-fi, but they've all got the sign. I had booked a room with a king-size bed, but they gave me two cots instead. "Same same but different," the clerk told me. This is the Nepali answer to everything. Cats and dogs? Same same but different. Freight trains and French fries? Same same but different.

Nepal is a tiny country packed with towering mountains. If it were flattened out, it would be the size of Africa, according to a fact I just made up. (With these mountains come constant landslides. As a result, bulldozer drivers are like rock stars here. When they come to town, farmers offer up their daughters for plowing.) It was one of these mountains that had drawn me here: Everest. It's not sexy like the Matterhorn or lyrical like Mt. Fuji. It's just tall and useless, like Yao Ming in the off-season. Beyond that, Everest is not much to look at: a plain white triangle, with all the grandeur and majesty of the corner of an envelope. And although it's the biggest thing on earth, it's nearly impossible to find – you can't even see Everest from Everest Base Camp! It's tucked deep in the Himalayas, so you have to climb another, better-looking mountain just to catch a glimpse of it. I was told it would be a four-hour trek. "Trek," I believe, is derived from the Yiddish word "dreck" meaning "a hike that's too awful to call it a hike." (NOTE: Nintety percent of what they call hikes are actually treks.)

I had an American friend named Wilson who helped set up the outing. He'd been here fifteen years, and gone Nepali nutso: He'd become a frantic mix of Dennis Hopper and Daffy Duck. And he claimed to speak the local language: "My friend-a here, he's-a want-a see Mount Everest." This was not Nepali, it was Jar Jar Binks English. "He's-a need a big walking stick much-much." A walking stick is a tool used by hikers. It provides the support and balance you need when carrying an ungainly six-foot piece of lumber. He made me spend fifty bucks on a stick to navigate a forest full of free sticks.

Wilson also hired a Sherpa to guide me, and as the man approached, I had an epiphany. The sights of Nepal are stunning, but the sounds and smells of the place are largely farts. There are thirty million Nepalis, and at any given moment, a third of them are in mid-fart. I blame it on a toxic combination of high altitude living and high-fiber diet. It gives a new interpretation to those paintings of Buddha (who was born in Nepal), fat and smiling, floating atop a cushion of green smoke.

I'm no fan of cheap flatulence jokes, and would let the subject pass (hey-hey!), except that it was a key part of the journey. As I followed my Sherpa up the steep mountain trail, he farted in my face with every step. Then, mercifully, he zoomed far off ahead of me, like a methane-fueled missile. His job as a Sherpa was to guide me, and thirty minutes into our four-hour climb, he had ceased sherping. I was lost and abandoned. I tossed aside my walking stick, greatly improving my mobility, and tried to find my way out.

And that's when I had Epiphany Number Two (Number Two – hey-hey!): Follow the cow dung. Cows come into the forest to graze, but they always return to their barns, pooping all the way. And any path a half-ton cow could manage worked for me. Yes, I followed farts into the forest and manure out of it. This was my vacation.

I came to an old logging road and followed its gentle slope up the mountain. The trip was peaceful, bucolic, and scenic. And I saw something I hadn't seen all morning: Nepalis. They knew better than to hike up a trail when they had a perfectly good road. I was greeted at every farmhouse with a cheerful "Namaste." I was at peace. The trek had become a hike.

I reached the mountaintop a few hours later. Shortly thereafter, my guide arrived. "How did you get here?" I asked.

"I followed you," he said. The Sherpa had become the Sherpee.

Later I found out he wasn't even a real Sherpa. Wilson, in his fractured English, had mistakenly hired a guy named Sherpa – it's a very common surname in Nepal. It's as if I needed a plumber and he brought me the corpse of Christopher Plummer. Same same but different.

Mr. Sherpa and I looked at each other, wondering what the hell we were doing up there. And then, just for a moment, the clouds parted, and we caught a glimpse of Everest. It was a crooked baby tooth of a mountain, a pimple on the nose of the Himalayas. It looked like a yogurt-covered raisin. But I'd seen it.

And suddenly I realized why I'd made this trip. The same reason men have always climbed mountains.

Because we're idiots.

Nepali Gothic

SIDE TRIP: Fear of Lying

You may be wondering, "Are all the crazy stories in this book true?"

And my answer is: absolutely. Sort of.

Sometimes I combine two good stories into one great one, a few times I've inserted myself into a story I wasn't really part of, and often I write myself something witty to say, when at the time, what I actually said was, "Goddammit, why did we spend all this money to come to this horrible place?"

But I never lie. Not that I don't want to, surely not that I have some moral objection to it… I just can't lie. I've never been good at it, not even as a kid. And children, bless their hearts, are lying little sacks of crap.

You might think my inability to lie would make me a great husband – for example, when I tell my wife she looks beautiful, she knows I mean it. But when she asks me, "Does this dress make my ass look fat?" Well, she learned long ago not to ask me things like that.

I'm telling you this because when you travel as much as I do, you're asked to lie constantly. For example, I was flying to Toronto to give a lecture, and my host told me, "When you get to the border, they'll ask if you're there for business or pleasure. Say pleasure – if you say business, they'll tie you up with paperwork for two hours."

That was the lie I had to tell. One word: "pleasure."

And yet, as I approached Canadian Border Control, I was sweating like I had a keister stuffed with heroin balloons.

The kindly border guard asked, "Are you here for business or pleasure?"

I'd been rehearsing the lie all night. ""PLEASURE!" I blurted.

"Wow, you came for pleasure, but you're only staying one night?"

I cracked under this relentless interrogation. "Okay it's business! I'm giving a speech at the Toronto UJA and even though it's a charity I'm getting paid one thousand two hundred and fifty dollars!"

About ninety minutes into filling out paperwork I realized he wasn't questioning me. He was being blandly friendly. He was being Canadian.

My next lie was on an actual pleasure trip to visit a friend in Copenhagen. He took me out to dinner at Noma, which for years had been ranked as the best restaurant in the world. When he saw me weaken and grow pale looking at the price list, he told me, "Don't worry – I'm paying for this."

I relaxed instantly, until he added, "But for tax purposes, you'll have to tell people you're my doctor."

I was unable to enjoy the meal that followed, worried that someone in the restaurant would start choking, someone else would yell, "Is there a doctor in the restaurant?" I'd have to stand up and say, "Yes! I'm pretending to be a doctor!"

This small lie ruined an amazing meal. One course was very rare reindeer steak, served with a hunting knife. The next course – and remember folks, I never lie to you – was clover, in dirt, served on a large rock.

"Do we eat the dirt?" I asked the waiter. He nodded.

"Do we eat the rock?" He shook his head. Sanity.

The dish was actually delicious, but I kept picturing the chef watching from the kitchen, laughing and elbowing the maître d': "I served them dirt on a rock and they ate it!"

A few years later my wife booked us a trip to Iraq, because, you know, she's crazy. I filled out my visa application listing my religion as Jewish – they ask your religion in "those countries" – and I listed my occupation as writer. The travel agent called in a tizzy: "They'll never let you into Iraq if you say you're a Jewish writer."

"Well, I'm not Isaac Bashevis Singer. I'm Jewish and a writer, and I'm not particularly good at either."

(By the way, that's one of those witty lines I thought up after. I think my actual response was, "Yippee! I'm not going to Iraq!")

The travel agent had been through this before. If I wanted to go to Iraq – and I didn't – I'd have to list myself as a Catholic publicist.

I told the travel agent I had no idea what a publicist does. I know what Catholics do, which is mostly stuff they're not supposed to do.

The travel agent said, "Don't worry. It will never come up."

It came up almost immediately. I hadn't even left the country – the clerk at Iraqi Air in New York was scrutinizing my visa. "So you're a publicist? What exactly do you do?"

"I… publicize things that need publicity. You know, basic PR."

"And what does PR stand for?"

"I don't know."

Denise continued our Axis of Evil Tour by booking a trip to North Korea. This time lying would not be a luxury but a necessity – that regime had repeatedly kidnapped visiting actors, writers, and directors, and forced them to make films for the government. Check out "Pulgasari" on YouTube: It's a North Korean rip-off of "Godzilla," made by a Chinese director who came to Pyongyang for a film festival and wound up as a hostage for eight years. I wouldn't fall into that trap. On my visa form, under "Occupation," I put "teacher," instead of what I was tempted to write: "comic genius." Two weeks later, the North Korean consulate called to tell us that they'd gone to China and Googled me, since North Korea has no internet. They found out who I was and what I've done, and that I was welcome to visit their country without fear. The implication was clear: They'd reviewed my writing credits and decided I wasn't worth kidnapping. I was pissed.

Denise has been known to lie herself. We were touring Honduras, and the highlight of the trip was a visit to a banana packaging center. The fact that this was the highlight tells you everything you need to know about Honduras and why you should avoid it like the plague. We arrived at Banana Central, only to be turned away by the gruff foreman. My wife cried, "Don't you know who I am? I'm Nicole Kidman!"

For the record, my wife is not Nicole Kidman, but she does resemble her more than, say, I do. It seemed like a real long shot, but it worked. The burly banana boxers ushered us in and were giving us a tour when their foreman put an end to this charade. Either he'd never heard of Nicole Kidman or, more likely, he was not a fan of her work.

I jumped in, naming the one celebrity I resemble. "Don't you know who I am? I'm the late Morey Amsterdam!"

We got tossed out.

Most recently, we lied to see a solar eclipse. Eclipses are great for the adventure traveler because they happen at random times in random places every year and a half – the last one was in Antarctica, the next one's in Texas. It's always a risky proposition. We went to Cairns, Australia for one eclipse and just as it began, a squat little cloud sailed in front of the sun, sat there for three solid minutes, then moved on just after the eclipse finished. It was timed like a Terry Gilliam cartoon, although he'd have had the cloud exit with a comical fart.

In 2020, the solar eclipse was visible in Argentina – a country that wasn't letting Americans in because of Covid. So my crafty wife signed us up for an expedition that was being allowed in. We just had to pretend to be scientists.

To review: In my career as a lying traveler, I've had to pose as a doctor, a teacher, a scientist, a publicist and a Catholic. These are all tough jobs. Why can't I pose as something easy, like a Wal-Mart greeter or a network TV executive?

The biggest problem with joining a science expedition is that you have to travel with real scientists. If they weren't talking about high-level astrophysics, they wouldn't say anything at all. Each morning I'd be greeted by silence when I asked them stumpers like, "Did you sleep well?" or "How was breakfast?" It was like being trapped for three days in an episode of "The Big Bang Theory." And I was the cute girl. Why must I always be the cute girl?

I was flattered when a young German scientist came to ME with a question. "I sent mein colleague a photo of me at the beach. He wrote back, 'I'm sorry the weather is so bad.' But the weather was not bad, it was beautiful. Why would he say this?"

I replied, "I think it was a joke."

"A joke." It seemed to be a new concept to him. Folks, unless you have a few hours to kill, don't try to explain a joke to an astrophysicist. Especially a German one.

The expedition began in beautiful, fun-filled Buenos Aires, but for the eclipse itself we'd be trucked to wind-blasted Patagonia – one of the worst places on earth. Four hours before the eclipse, we were dumped in an open horse pasture, with no shelter from the gale force winds. Denise and I tried to explore the area, but the field was ankle-deep in thorns and horse manure. This was my Sophie's Choice – step in thorns to avoid horse crap or step in horse crap to avoid thorns. Of course there's going to be horse manure in a horse pasture, but it was shocking to see great piles and pyramids of it everywhere. This was Argentina's Strategic Horse Crap Reserve.

And then at 1:08 p.m., all of this ceased to matter. The moon crept in front of the sun, the sky faded from midday brightness to midnight blue, the scientists gurgled in nerdy delight, and the horses stopped crapping. They were literally scared shitless. For two minutes and six seconds, the sun was an eerie black circle you could stare straight at. It was so wrong and so beautiful. I was even grateful to those Patagonia winds for keeping the clouds at bay

It was all worth it. All the expense, all the travel, all the lying, all that horse crap, just for two minutes of pure excitement.

"Sounds like our honeymoon."

Ha ha. That was my wife – now she's lying.

"I'm not lying."

Denise tried to get into a banana farm claiming to be Nicole Kidman. It didn't work.

Chapter 8

WHAT AM I DOING IN THE MUSLIM WORLD?

Fun-Filled Iran

When my wife was a kid, she took a round-the-world trip, visiting poor countries, dirty countries, dangerous countries, until she reached the promised land: a nation of luxury, wealth, and sophistication. A place… called Iran.

This was Iran in the '70s, ruled by the Shah. The Shah was a brutal dictator, but back then he was OUR brutal dictator, and Iran was the Paris of the Middle East. In fact, they still say "Merci" for "thank you."

About ten years ago, at the height of US/Iranian tensions, my wife said she wanted to go back for a visit.

"No," I said.

"No?" she replied, baffled. My wife speaks five languages, but couldn't seem to understand this.

"No," I repeated. "Their government supports terrorism, Holocaust denial, and the oppression of women. So, no, I am not going to Iran. And if you have any respect for me, you won't ever ask again."

A few weeks later, we were on a plane bound for Iran. I was surrounded by Iranian nationals and they all looked like me: dark curly hair, dark eyes, more nose than was strictly necessary. They may have been anti-semites, but they were still semites.

Midway through the flight, my wife asked, "How long do you think we'll be in Iran before someone speaks to you in Farsi?"

I said, "It already happened when I got up to use the bathroom."

So, we were headed to a country full of friendly, very good-looking people. Maybe it wouldn't be so bad.

The second we landed, we were taken into custody. They sequestered us in a dingy room at the airport. There were two officials there – one offered us tea and honey cake. It was like being held hostage by grandma.

After two hours, they let us go. They never questioned us, they never looked at our paperwork. "What was that all about?" I asked.

"I don't know," said one official. "But you do it to us when we come to your country."

Our tour guide was a long-haired, laid-back, twentyish Tehrani. He asked me what I did for a living. How could I explain "The Simpsons" to a young man who'd never left Iran? Do they have cartoons there? Do they even have TV?

I began, "I write for this show called "The Simpsons'…"

He replied, "I really liked the early seasons."

This kid was full of surprises. He told me he had just been to a Blue Oyster Cult concert.

"Really?" I had to ask him: "Do you have drugs here?" I asked.

"Sure. Pot, speed, coke, acid… what do you need?"

"The Simpsons," drugs, mediocre '70s rock bands – it's amazing what parts of American culture the Middle East has latched onto. They love Gabriel Iglesias, aka Fluffy, the plus-size Hispanic comedian. And they're big fans of ventriloquist Jeff Dunham –they particularly enjoy his puppet Achmed the Dead Terrorist. Go figure.

And the Middle East is crazy about the American West. One beloved actor is spaghetti Western star Bud Spencer. Who? He played the beefy lug in dozens of films, such as "God Forgives… I Don't" and "Even Angels Eat Beans." He also starred in the TV show "Detective Extralarge." That was his last name: Extralarge. Though Arabs think he's American, Bud Spencer was actually Italian water polo star Carlo Pedresoli. He named himself after two Americans he loved: the Spencer from Spencer Tracy and the Bud from Budweiser beer.

A favorite American TV show in the Middle East is "Caught in Providence." It's a YouTube version of The People's Court featuring an obscure Rhode Island judge named Frank Caprio.

"He is so wise, your Judge Caprio," one tour guide told me. "I use his videos to raise my children."

What the falafel?

I've mentioned before that Tehran is exactly like Los Angeles: the traffic, the smog, the large number of Iranians. Still, sharia law was in effect: Women, including my wife, had to dress in head scarves and long skirts or pants. Still, those who wanted to look attractive found ways around it: elaborate eye make-up and bangs, beautiful manicures, filmy hijabs, and clingy jilbabs. My guide nudged me as a woman walked by: "Hey Mike, did you see the wrists on her?"

When I tell Iranian Americans I visited their country they're always delighted. "That's wonderful. It is a beautiful country. How long were you there?"

I say eighteen days.

"Eighteen days? That's too long."

It was too long. Everywhere we went, we'd visit the local madrassa or school, the bazaar, and the hamam or ritual bath. They were all nice and they were all exactly the same. And every meal was giant piles of kababs, French fries, and rice. Their national dish is A LOT.

We also visited dozens of beautiful mosques, all gilded, filled with colorful mosaics, mirrors, and chandeliers. Islam forbids making pictures of people, so a mosque is not like a church: You're not bummed out by paintings of saints being whipped or shot with arrows or grilled alive. The job of a mosque is to be lovely and they hit the mark pretty often.

I can't say the same for the local hotels, but I blame our travel agent for that. We were staying in a real dump in the holy city of Moshad, surrounded by six square blocks of auto parts stores. I had to take a long bus ride to get to the heart of town, where I spotted a four-star luxury hotel. "Nice place," I said to a guest in the lobby.

He replied, "It should be – I'm paying forty dollars a night!"

We made one more special visit. Not too far out of Tehran, not too far off the road, our cab driver pulled off into the desert. He showed us three huge concrete circles in the sand. "See that? Under there, we're enriching uranium for nuclear weapons!" Fun stop. After that we went out for Iranian ice cream.

We visited every corner of Iran: Qom, Koy, Kajan, Yazd, Bam... many Iranian cities are named after punch noises from the old Batman show. Bam's name was particularly ironic since the entire city collapsed – BAM! – in a 2003 earthquake. Even the city's famous ruins were in ruins. But despite our strained relations with Iran, the US government and its people gave generously to aid earthquake relief. Did you know Americans are the statistically most charitable people on earth? And they adopt as many children as the rest of the world combined?

You know who knows that? Iranians. They like Americans. They like our movies, our TV, our rock and roll. Everyone in Iran has a cousin who came to America and found success as a doctor, an engineer, or Christiane Amanpour.

And they're pretty generous people themselves. I visited a mosque and on the way out they forced me to take two crates of juice boxes. I stuck my nose into a clothing store and walked out with a free men's suit, tailored to fit me. Need to get somewhere? Just hold out your hand. A passing driver will pick you up, and if he's heading in the right direction, take you closer. Two or three hops like this will get you anywhere you want to go. So to any children listening: If you're in an enemy country, always take rides from strangers.

And then there was the Feast of Imam Hussein. It's a sad holiday commemorating the martyrdom of Muhammud's grandson. Women wail and slap their chests. Men walk the streets, whipping themselves with chains. But not too hard. I've had massages that were more painful. The fact is that the Iranians are like my people the Jews: There's no holiday so sad that you can't make a banquet out of it. Strangers invited us into their home for a huge chicken and rice dinner. As we were leaving, they handed us two more chicken dinners to go. Who else keeps to-go cartons in their home?

As I walked the teeming streets, filled with wailing women and whipping dudes, more strangers handed me chicken dinners. Soon, I was overburdened, carrying as many meals as I could handle. I looked like a Christmas tree decorated with chicken dinners. And one little boy invited me to his home for dinner. When I turned him down, he said, "You are from America?"

I said yes. He asked, "Do you know Judge Caprio?"

My final meal of the trip was with some friends of friends in Northern Tehran, the Beverly Hills of Iran. They had a big beautiful home and it featured something I hadn't seen for eighteen days: booze. Alcohol's illegal in Iran, but, like America's Prohibition, if you want it, you can get it. This family had a personal bootlegger who brought top-shelf liquor to their back door at night. Some of it looked a little… fake, including Marker's Make Bourbon and a brand of vodka called Absolutely. More surprising than seeing liquor, I was shocked when our hostess came into the dining room without a head scarf. I hadn't seen a woman's hair in more than two weeks. If she'd walked in naked from the waist down, I couldn't have been more scandalized. Clearly, it was time for me to leave Iran. After a lovely dinner, the family gave us two more dinners to take with us.

That was a decade ago, and since then I've been begging my wife to go back to Iran. She says no.

"No?" I say incredulous. I miss the people, the sights, and the amazing hospitality. Plus, we finally ate the last chicken dinner.

Half-ing Fun in Jordan

If Iran still sounds a little intense for you, ease into the Middle East with a trip to Jordan. This country feels so much like America you may wonder why you bothered to visit. Some of this may stem from the king – his name's Abdullah bin Hussein bin Talal bin Abdullah – yes, it's got an Abdullah at both ends – but he's about as Jordanian as a Dunkin' Donuts. His mother was English, and came to Jordan as a production secretary on "Lawrence of Arabia." This guy went to high school in Massachusetts and college in Britain, and when he became king he couldn't even speak Arabic.

Still, there's one very compelling reason to visit Jordan – Petra. It's been featured in roughly ten thousand Nat Geo specials. If you missed those, you'll remember Petra from the third "Raiders" movie, "Indiana Jones and the Old Cup," or whatever it was. That movie ends with Indy, played by Han Solo, and his father, played by James Bond, riding off into the desert. They stop at an amazing church carved right out of a red sandstone cliff. That's Petra. People think that's the whole thing, but when you go around the corner you see it continues for another hundred square miles. It's an entire city carved out of pure rock, bright red and beautiful. It's two thousand years old and looks like it was just finished yesterday. Petra should be number three on your bucket list, after the Pyramids and the Great Wall of China. Number four should be finding the schmuck who coined the term "bucket list" and hitting him with a bucket.

Beyond Petra, there's not a lot to see in Jordan. One big attraction is Wadi Rum, which is a vast chunk of desert inside a much bigger desert. A wadi is a dried riverbed, so they're basically taking you to see a river that isn't there. When we reached Wadi Rum, the host offered us tea – I don't like tea, and my wife doesn't drink it at all, but we took it to be polite. I had to choke down both cups, at which point our host said, "Please, take more, take more." So I wound up drinking four cups of tea I didn't want. We spent a freezing cold night in the wadi doing nothing, and the next morning the ritual repeated: I was cajoled into drinking another two cups, and then two more. Then, as I was leaving, our host charged me sixty-four bucks for eight cups of tea. Not the Arab hospitality I was used to.

In fact, we noticed something truly strange about the Jordanians – no matter what you asked for, they gave you half. If a city tour was supposed to visit six sites, it went to three. A four-course meal was only two courses. We were booking a day trip, and they asked if we wanted the two-hour hike or the three-hour hike. We paid for three hours and the hike lasted ninety minutes. It was actually shorter than a two-hour hike except their two-hour hike would've been an hour.

We could only laugh about it. It gave rise to a bunch of Jordan jokes:

What was showing at the Jordanian film festival?

-"The Five Commandments"

-"Snow White and the Three-and-a-Half Dwarfs"

-Federico Fellini's classic film "Four and a Quarter"

And here's my best Jordan joke:

Who's their favorite rapper?

Fifty Percent

Those Wacky Iraqis

We took a trip to the safe area of Iraq, which is like visiting the Jewish area of South Dakota. For the record, there are two hundred fifty Jews in that enormous state, comprising zero percent of the population.

As for the safe part of Iraq, that's a tiny region called Kurdistan. It borders the mountains of Iran so it is literally between Iraq and a hard place. What a great joke! I should stop right there.

Kurdistan is a semi-autonomous region run by Kurds: They have their own language, they police their own borders, everyone knows everyone because everyone's related to everyone. It's almost modern and almost peaceful, like Arizona. It looks like Arizona, too: vast stretches of desert, craggy mountains, and buttes, deep winding river canyons. If Italy could make spaghetti westerns, you could shoot Falafel Westerns here: "A Fistful of Dinars"; "The Good, the Bad, and the Burqa"; "Gunfight at the OK Koran"; "The Man Who Shot Libyan Violence." None of these are good, so I gave you a lot of them. Here's one that doesn't even make sense: "Al Qaeda on the Western Front."

We stayed in the capital city of Erbil, in a lovely hotel popular with American spies: They were well-dressed men who sat in the bar all day, nursing a single drink, eavesdropping on conversations around them. Maybe they weren't spies. Maybe they were just nosey, lazy, and bored. By the way, Nosey, Lazy & Bored is a great name for a budget law firm:

"Nosey, Lazy & Bored: That Bench Isn't Just Our Ad – It's Our Office."

Kurdistan felt safe – so safe they built Iraq's first American-style mall. It was a shiny, spotless '80s mall, right out of "Stranger Things." And it had something most Iraqis had never seen before: an escalator. It was cute watching the Kurds navigate this thing: waiting forever before they stepped aboard, wobbling and clutching the rubber railing for dear life on the ride down, and stumbling and being thrown off at the bottom. For most of them, the escalator ride was much scarier than the war going on outside their borders. We also went to a local zoo, where there were no guards. Kids climbed into the monkey cages for selfies. Teens pulled on a lion's whiskers.

Fun and fear sit side by side in Iraq. One night, we were riding a Ferris wheel – Iraq has lots of amusement parks because Iraqis have lots of kids: 4.6 per household, the most in the world. It was all fun until we reached the top of the Ferris wheel – we could see into Mosul, the next city over, where all hell was breaking loose.

Still, we felt safe in Kurdistan. How safe? One day a black sedan with tinted windows pulled up to us. The passenger door opened up and the driver said, "Get in." So we got in! There was an old man behind the wheel – he just wanted to practice his English. He lamented, "When I was boy, everyone here could speak English. Now it's just BALALALA." He gave us a tour of the town then dropped us off at a beautiful church – the last church on earth still giving services in Aramaic. That's the language Jesus spoke. It was like listening to the original cast album of the New Testament.

But there was still danger. The week before, two hundred Christians had been gunned down in an Egyptian church. Our church was being protected by an eighty-year-old man holding a machine gun he couldn't quite lift. When we left the church, he was holding it by the barrel, using it to knock lemons out of a tree.

SIDE TRIP: Dirty Jokes from The Muslim World

had a driver in Saudi Arabia who had a great joke he just had to tell me: "Why did the foolish man bring a spoon to sleep? So he could eat rice with the angels! (LAUGHS) He is eating rice with the angels! You can use that on your show!"

My tour guide leaned over to me and explained that the driver's joke made sense in Arabic, but lost something in translation. In fact, it lost EVERYTHING in translation. None of this stopped the driver. He had a million of 'em! All bad.

"A little boy asked his uncle for a gift. So the uncle shoved a date up his butt."

This was less a joke than a case for social services.

Some of the jokes at least made sense. For example, if you see a man in Saudi Arabia with lots of kids, you say, "He must have no electricity." Get it? No electricity means no TV, no computers, no distractions. That means sex, and sex means kids.

Other jokes made sense as long as you knew a few things. For example, in the Muslim world, Friday and Saturday are the weekend. Their Thursday is like our Friday, and our "Thank God It's Friday" is their "Praise Allah, It's Thursday." And Thursday night means sex, and nobody loves sex like the Egyptians. Got it? And now the joke:

"For Egyptian men, every night is Thursday night."

Saudi Arabians have another kind of joke, that's actually funny and like nothing I've ever heard:

"Mike! How do you put an elephant in an empty refrigerator?"

"I don't know."

"You can't. If the elephant's in it, it's not empty. Mike! The lion had a birthday party. Every animal in the jungle came to it except for one. Which one?"

"I give up."

"The elephant! He was still stuck in the refrigerator."

You get the pattern. Sometimes they had a string of these, six riddles long.

I even heard a joke from the Koran. There's jokes in the Koran!

Muhammud and his uncle are eating dates. His uncle puts all his date pits on top of Muhammud's date pits, and says, "Look how hungry you were!"

Muhammud points to his uncle's empty plate and says, "You were even hungrier. You ate all your dates AND the pits!"

Before you dismiss that, tell me your favorite joke from the Bible. There are none! No jokes in either Testament. And they were written by Jews!

Still the joke I'll never forget was the one our German guide Erica told a tour group in Hamburg:

"A sailor is scrrrrewing whore. Und the sailor says, "How am I doing?" She said, "You're doing three knots. You're not in, you're not hard, and you're not getting your fifty Deutch Marks' back."

That joke really made me laugh. Particularly because she told it to a group of Baptist ministers.

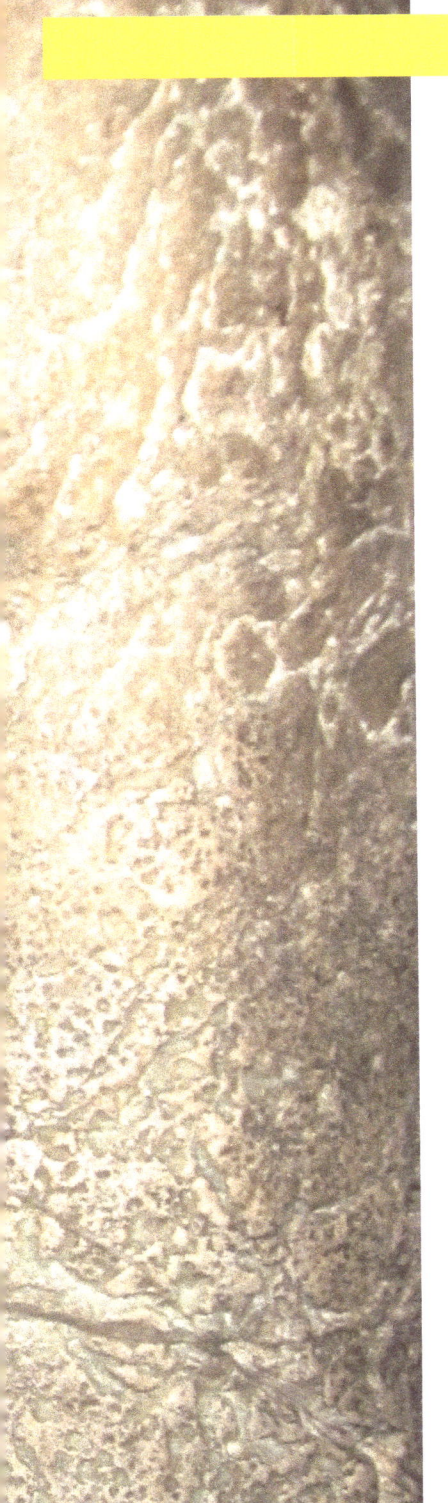

Chapter 9

THREE PLACES TO DIE BEFORE YOU GO

Since this is mostly a book of complaints, you won't see much about the nice vacations I've had. You won't read about Australia, because they've never given me anything to carp about. I've been there six times, to six different regions, and always had a wonderful time. Australia is just like America, only a little better. It's America 2.0. We're friendly, they're friendlier. We love beer, they worship it. Both nations were founded around the same time, an ocean away from snooty old England. But America was established by religious zealots – Australia was built by convicts. That's why they're more fun.

And Myanmar is the loveliest, most tranquil country I ever visited. Their president even won the Nobel Peace Prize. Not long after, though, she was accused of committing genocide in her own country. She's currently in prison awaiting trial. Ethiopia's president also won the Peace Prize and is also accused of genocide. It's like they think, "I won the Nobel Peace Prize, baby! Time to be a total dick."

I have nothing but good things to say about Canada, Ireland, Thailand, Sri Lanka, and even pre-civil war Syria, so they don't appear in this book. However, I have saved the worst for near-last: What follows are three of the most awful places I've ever been. Enjoy my misery.

Slaughterhouse Five-Star Hotel

If there were a Museum of Bad Ideas, the main exhibit would be ... well, the museum itself. It's a terrible concept. But the second-worst idea might be this: "Let's turn an old industrial slaughterhouse into a luxury hotel!" The problem is not that someone tried this – it's that they didn't try hard enough. From the outside, this posh resort in southern Chile looks like a death camp, because that's what it was – a century ago, up to two hundred fifty thousand sheep were butchered here – each year! To access the hotel's Zen spa, you have to walk through the same concrete chute thousands of lambs were funneled through on their trip to the stockyards. To get to their elegant dining room, you have to pass through the Gallery of Carnage: a cavernous, drafty hall decorated with sepia photos of lambs being skinned and hung on hooks. Bon appetit!

If I were a vegan, this place would be the Ritz Auschwitz. But even though I love eating little lambs, this place still creeped me out. My room was cozy and beautifully appointed, but when I lay down in bed, I could see they'd kept the old abattoir ceiling: rusty steel plates with a single bare bulb hanging from a wire. The decor was an uncomfortable mix of "Downton Abbey" and "Saw."

Another problem with this hotel – and it really didn't need another problem –was that every single employee in every single department was bad at their job: reception, housekeeping, and especially the bar staff. Every night I'd order a cerveza just to see what they'd bring: a whiskey sour, a bowl of peanuts, nothing, a cup of coffee, the hotel manager – anything but a beer. Ordering became a Dada exercise.

There were sheep who had a better time here than me.

Of course, it's hard to find good help when you build your hotel in one of the least-populated spots on the planet: Patagonia. But with its snow-capped mountains, crystal-blue rivers, and sweeping golden plains, there's no place quite like Patagonia. Except Montana. And Colorado. And Utah. And Idaho, I imagine. But Patagonia has one thing they don't have: persistent gale-force winds. The wind blows all the freaking time, and like Patagonia itself, it blows hard.*

The travel agent who sent us here neglected to mention this. But everyone else couldn't stop talking about it:

TOUR GUIDE: This was the last place on earth man settled in, due to the high winds…

FJORD CRUISE CAPTAIN: There are at least three reasons for Patagonia's high winds…

HOTEL CLERK: You might wear these earplugs to bed to block the noise of the high winds…

It's windy because there's no other land at this latitude. Even Pangaea knew not to come here. If you don't believe me, look at a map. (You're not gonna look at a map.) All the wind in the lower Southern Hemisphere hits Patagonia, because there is nothing else on earth to stop it. It's a great place to visit, if you're a kite.

When I called the travel agent to complain, she said, "Patagonia is lovely, except for the wind." Which is like saying, "Lung cancer is a lot of fun, except for the cancer." (In fact, the tobacco companies have said just that.)

So why do people travel here? It's the name: Patagonia. It sounds so romantic one friend asked me, "You mean that's a real place?" Of course, the name loses a little in translation. It's like the Bolshoi Ballet: It sounds so classy, but bolshoi just means "big.' Bolshoi Ballet? Big Ballet. Big deal.

According to legend, when Magellan first visited Patagonia, he saw an Indian's huge footprint in the snow – the natives stood almost a foot taller than the European invaders. "These people have feet like ducks (patos)," Magellan is said to have remarked. "Let's kill them all."

Patagonia? Terrific name for a sportswear company. Land of People with Duck Feet? Not so much.

Patagonia has lovely glaciers you can cruise by, but to reach the tour boat, you have to walk across a mile-wide valley where the winds gust at eighty MPH. The gales literally blew my mouth open and began inflating me like a party balloon. When I finally reached the boat, the captain told me, "The water's a little rough today, but don't worry, we have a plan B." A few minutes later, the trip was canceled due to (brace yourself) high winds.

"So what's Plan B?" I asked.

"We have no Plan B," he replied.

There is, in fact, just one other tourist attraction here. It's called Tres Torres– three giant black squares of rock jutting out of a mountaintop. To me, they looked like something out of Dante: Satan's rotting teeth. It's a four-hour, near-vertical climb to reach the Devil's Dentures, with the wind pushing you back at each step. Everything about this place said, "Don't go there." My wife wanted to go there.

A good husband would never send his wife on this life-threatening hike alone, so clearly I suck. Denise and I have been together for three decades; we could spend one random day apart. This random day happened to be December 25th.

My wife spent Christmas making this grueling climb, while I remained in comfort at the Abattoir Suites Hotel. That's where I wrote this story, while enjoying an ice-cold cerveza. Of course, what I'd ordered was a club sandwich.

'To be honest, the wind stops blowing during the winter, when Patagonia is too cold to visit. But when summer comes and the suckers return, the warm air rises creating a vacuum, which is filled by cold gusting winds from nearby Antarctica. This has inspired my new comedy series '"It's Always Sucky in Patagonia."

North Korea? Really?

"You went to North Korea? You? How did YOU get in there?"

North Korea's the second most surprising place I've been to, after Harvard.

"You went to Harvard? You? How did YOU get in there?"

Harvard and North Korea are pretty similar institutions: scary places run by evil men, completely cut off from the real world. In fact, Harvard is the reason I visited North Korea. I woke up one morning to see an email from Harvard Alumni Travel Experience, or H.A.T.E. It was an invitation to join a three-day trip to North Korea. I did not want to go, but I knew my wife would, so I deleted the email before she saw it.

But when Denise woke up, she got the same email from Harvard Travel. Yes, my wife studied there, too. In fact, there are only two things I took away from Harvard that I treasure to this day: my wife and a pile of library books. They're both stacked in the bedroom.

AUDIENCE: BOOOO!

Who are you people?

Denise, of course, was excited to visit North Korea. This was during the reign of Kim Jong-il, the chubby crazy dictator with the bad haircut; he was the father of their current ruler Kim Il-Sung, a chubbier, crazier man with an even worse haircut. Though the North Korean nuclear program continues to sputter, they lead the world in lousy hairdos.

As I've mentioned earlier, there was extra danger in me visiting North Korea: their ruler Kim Jong-il loved show business. He wrote treatises on cinema and owned twenty thousand movies on DVD. If he weren't a ruthless dictator, he would've made a great Blockbuster Video Manager. But Kim had the unfortunate habit of kidnapping visiting actors, directors, and writers and forcing them to make films for his regime. On the other hand, as a sixty-year-old TV writer, abduction was my best shot at a career.

Still, I urged Denise not to book the trip, and still she booked it. A few weeks later, we got a call from the North Korean Embassy. They examined my credits and determined I was no threat to their government. Anyone who'd worked for Fox as long as I had knew how to respect an Evil Empire. They asked only that I never write about the trip. Well, I'm doing it now folks. If Kim Jong-Un is reading this book, I'm screwed.

North Korea does not usually let Americans in. But for three weeks a year, they stage a spectacle so spectacular they have to share it with the world. It's called the Mass Games, and it's like the Olympics Opening Ceremony, without any Olympics behind it. You see, North Korea doesn't believe in the Olympics – as a Communist country, they think we're all equal and competition is a bad thing. But that doesn't mean they can't be fabulous!

The government built a three-day package around the Mass Games. Whether you're a tourist, a journalist or Dennis Rodman, you all get the same trip. And you all stay in the same hotel – it's dreary high-rise in North Korea's capital city Pyongyang. The hotel has one notable feature – a moat. I'm not kidding – the hotel is situated on a man-made island in the middle of town, and you can't go anywhere. We joined a group of fourteen hardy travelers, and we had seven government minders watching us all day long.

No one in the group knew each other – we were random strangers united by a love of truly stupid vacations. One man in our group was…The Most Traveled Man on Earth. You might think that title would go to some famous explorer or a career diplomat. But no, it was just a chubby schlub in a "Star Wars" T-shirt. He may have been a math teacher in Queens, but he was the man who'd been everywhere. My wife could not resist grilling him:

DENISE: Have you been to Libya?

GUY: Yes.

DENISE: Afghanistan?

GUY: Yes.

DENISE: Siberia?

GUY: Ten times.

DENISE: Ten times?

GUY: Every time you go, you see something different.

Pause

DENISE: Have you been to Cameroon?

GUY: We can play this game all day. I've been everywhere.

Depending on how you look at it, Pyongyang is either a world-class city or the most depressing place on earth. It's criss-crossed by stately boulevards ten lanes wide. But the streets are empty because no one can afford a car. Our tour bus driver liked to pinball down the highway, zig-zagging across five lanes from one side to the other. Why? Because he could.

Who needs roads anyway? Pyongyang has a subway system, where the stations look like French chateaux, filled with fine art, murals, and chandeliers. It's built on the Stalinist philosophy that trains should have better homes than the people do.

The city has an impressive skyline of high-rises, but at night they go pitch-black. No electricity. Towering over the city was a hundred-and-five story hotel that loomed, half-finished, for nineteen years. It made it into the Guinness Book as the tallest unoccupied building in the world. It was intended to a symbol of the city, and in a way, it is.

It would be easy to say everything's horrible there, but it's not quite true. The people are all skinny and shabbily dressed, but their life expectancy is about the same as ours, and their health care system is probably better. Pyongyang has impossibly beautiful public parks filled with picnicking families. I got pulled into an impromptu folk dance by some old ladies who were dressed in vibrant floral robes and drunk off their asses.

But the big attraction of the city is its monuments: the hundred-foot-tall Arch of Reunification; giant bronze sculptures of Kim Jong-Il and Kim Il-Sung. There's the Monument to Party Founding ten stories tall; it's a sculpture of three giant fists clutching a hammer, a paintbrush, and what looks like a backscratcher. And they built an Arc de Triomphe based on the one in Paris but jussst a little bigger. There are giant statues everywhere you turn: Imagine all the monuments in Washington D.C. jammed into downtown Bethesda.

However, you have to drive twenty minutes outside Pyongyang to see their greatest memorial: the grave of the nation's founder Kim Il-Sung. It's the largest tomb of any Communist leader, so suck, it, Mao-Tse Tung. The Mausoleum is called Kumsusan Palace and it has corridors over a kilometer long. I'd say it looks like an airport, but the tomb is actually much larger than North Korea's main

Airport in Pyongyang. (When I Googled to confirm this, the number one question that popped up was, "Does Pyongyang Airport have a TGI Fridays?" The answer is NOOOO!)

The Mausoleum sits atop a gorgeously landscaped hill and is equal parts memorial and theme park ride. You stand on a conveyor belt and roll through rooms filled with portraits and statues of the dear leader. My favorite was the Hall of Lamentations, where loudspeakers blast people's memories of Kim Il-Sung over a soundtrack of loud wailing: "When our Supreme Leader died, people cried non-stop for eighteen days. Our streets were flooded in tears up to our waistlines." It's not subtle. But it works. North Korean visitors around me were sobbing.

Next the conveyor belt carries you through an air-blaster that blows dirt off of you; it's basically a carwash for human grief. And finally you get to see the man himself – Kim Il-Sung lies in a giant glass coffin. Guards instruct you to bow three times and then exit through the gift shop. The whole experience takes forty-five minutes; that's the equivalent of five Haunted Mansion rides followed by four Pirates of the Caribbean.

What can I say: Kim Jong-il put together a pretty snappy tour: riverboat rides, Paper Lantern Festivals, and a visit to the DMZ. Every meal was a banquet and one featured dog soup. I didn't have the heart to eat it, but another tourist did. He said, "It has bite."

AUDIENCE: BOOOO!

Oh, you guys are back.

It was finally time for the main event, the festival that had brought us to North Korea – the Mass Games. I'd expected some sort of Socialist Parade – soldiers marching in formation; giant missiles rolling by on flatbed trucks; women in welding suits riding tractors. Instead, it was pure Vegas: Eighty thousand gymnasts in spangled outfits, doing dance routines to disco music; there were fireworks and thousands of synchronized hula hoopers. In case this wasn't impressive enough, thirty thousand children sat in the stands opposite us. They put on a "card show," flipping large placards to form giant pictures of their country, its monuments, and its leaders. The card show never stopped and not one kid messed up. There were a dozen costume changes all seamlessly choreographed: Ten thousand dancers in mermaid costumes would slip off the field as ten thousand more came on dressed in sailor suits.

The show lasted ninety minutes TO THE SECOND and it truly was the most jaw-dropping spectacle I've ever seen. When I left the stadium, I learned something that made it even more impressive:

although the spectators had a roof over their heads, the performers on field did not. They had just performed that flawless extravaganza for us in a pounding rainstorm.

Still, I saw something even more remarkable on my last day in North Korea. We stopped to see an indoor circus at a local theater. It was a depressing array of acts. This was Cirque du Socialism, performed in a dingy living room set right out of "Death of a Salesman." But the final performer was an actual bear who walked out on her hind legs – and vacuumed. She used a real upright vacuum cleaner, and she didn't miss a spot. She vacuumed under the table, the chairs, the sofa – stuff my cleaning lady never does. If that bear is reading this book and I truly hope she is: Honey, if you ever want to give up show business, you can clean my place twice a week.

The question I always hear about North Korea was "How did you get in there?" The question I got most in SOUTH Korea was, "What are you doing here?" South Koreans seemed absolutely baffled why anyone would visit their country. It's the same question I got when Jennifer Aniston found me in her living room: "What are you doing here?" In that case, my answer was, "If you didn't want intruders, why is your security code 1234?"

I'm just kidding. I don't know where Jennifer Aniston lives. This was Courtney Cox's living room.

There are, in fact, many reasons to visit South Korea. They have better roads and faster internet than any other country. Their people are better educated than us and they live longer than anyone. They will literally bury us all.

Their long lives may be due to their perfect mix of hard work and joie de vivre. It's like they combine German industry and Italian joy. That's probably better than Italian industry and German joy. Am I right?

I'm not right.

You can't make those jokes anymore. I apologize.

Their cities are spotless and futuristic: They have two indoor amusement parks, built inside skyscrapers, on the same block! I also visited the Hello Kitty Museum, three teddy bear museums, and the Sculpture Park of Giant Erotic Art. Oh, they also have historic temples and villages, if you like that sort of thing. And outside the cities are mountains as spiky and green as pineapple tops.

South Korea is where they made the movie "Parasite" and animate "The Simpsons." They also gave us K-pop music, which is such a powerful cultural export, it's underwritten by the Korean

government. They call it "soft power." Why bomb your enemies when you can bombard them with boy bands?

The food is delicious AND healthy AND cheap! The hat trick! Order any meal, and it'll come with a dozen tiny side dishes, all free… all kimchi. This is South Korea's national dish – it's pickled cabbage served in two hundred different ways. You may only know it from an episode of MASH, where a pot of kimchi stinks up the whole army base. In truth, kimchi stinks a little, but so do those last few seasons of MASH. Am I right?

I'm not right. I can't make those jokes either.

South Korea is probably one of my favorite Koreas. It's got great sights, great food, great people. So why were they shocked to see me there? Because they don't need tourists. They've got a beautiful place and they want to keep it to themselves. Just like Courteney Cox's living room.

That's a joke… too. It was David Schwimmer's.

Erotic sculpture park, South Korea.

Worst Vacation Ever!

There are things you saw over and over in old comedies that you never saw in real life.

I never saw a Boy Scout help an old lady across the street. I never saw a woman jump on a chair when she saw a mouse. I never saw a woman faint when she saw a mouse and be revived with smelling salts – back then, everyone seemed to carry smelling salts. Now, we don't even know what they are.

I never saw a woman hit her husband with a rolling pin. I never saw a drunk talking to a lamppost. I never saw a guy with a toothache wear a towel wrapped around his head and tied in a bow at the top. What was that for?

I've visited the poorest countries on earth, but never met anyone so broke they were wearing a barrel.

And in all my visits to the world's jungles and deserts, I never saw quicksand. It was in cartoons, in sitcoms, in dramas, in action movies. It seemed to be everywhere. Well, guess what? Quicksand does exist, but it's extremely rare and completely impossible to get sucked under it.

There are things in comedy that do exist, but in real life THEY'RE NOT FUNNY AT ALL. I once slipped on a banana peel – classic comedy, right? Except when I did it, I tore a groin muscle. Not amusing to me. Hilarious to you, I'm sure. Grow up.

My neighbor once fell down a manhole –it messed her up for life. In Kazakhstan, I did something I'd only seen in cartoons – I fell through a stairway that had a missing step. I wound up, feet dangling, supported by my armpits. Not funny, man. And I suffer from sciatica – you know, that comedy disease where Grampa says, "Oh, my sciatica's acting up." Guess what? Sciatica hurts like hell!

Finally, in Honduras, I was chased out of a restaurant by an angry chef with a meat cleaver. I'd seen this in a million cartoons, but trust me: When it happens to you, it's scary. My tour director had parked me at this cozy bistro with the assurance: "The meal has been paid for in advance. Drinks included."

"Even beer?" I asked.

"Anything."

"Including beer?"

"BEER IS OKAY!"

To be safe, I cleared it again with the waiter. "I can order a beer and there will be no charge?"

"There will be no charge. Everything is paid for."

I didn't even want a beer, but it was free, so I ordered one. And at the end of the meal, I got charged for it. I told the waiter. "Hey! You said beer was included!"

"No, senor, soft drinks are included. Beer is extra."

"I'm not paying for this," I said.

He went to the kitchen to discuss this with his boss, and a moment later, an old lady came charging out of the back, waving a meat cleaver and screaming at me in Spanish. The sad part is, this is still one of the better meals I had in Honduras. The country's national cuisine is Appleby's, Pizza Hut, and Chinese food on Sundays. And service is not really their strong suit – I walked into a Chinese place that was dead empty except for seven waiters standing in a corner, smoking. No one came over to me, no one even acknowledged my presence. For an hour.

I've been to one hundred and thirty-four countries. When people ask me my worst trip, I tell them, "My vacations are like my children. There are some I hate much more than others." But if I were ranking my worst trip, Honduras would definitely be in the top one. I'm not alone in this. In fact, the first out-of-towner to have a bad visit there was Christopher Columbus. "Honduras" means "depths," and as Columbus left, he coined the name for the country: "Gracias a Dios que hemos salido de esas Honduras." Which means, "Thank God we have departed from those depths." That was their first Yelp review. If they put it on T-shirts, I'd buy one.

There are reasons to visit the Honduras. They have a beautiful island off the coast called Roatan; you can fly directly in and out of the place without visiting the mainland. That's its attraction: it's a trip to Honduras wherever you never set foot in Honduras.

There's also Mayan ruins in Copan that are not to be missed. That's why we went to Honduras; then the tour guide persuaded my wife to book an extra week to see the rest of the country.

Big mistake. Every hotel clerk I met was crabby; the rooms leaked water, and the beaches were covered with nails and broken glass. Oh yeah, and I got kidnapped. I have so many complaints, I often forget that one. And I don't blame Honduras: It was never meant to be a tourist destination. For over a century, their business was bananas. In fact, O. Henry coined a term when referring to Honduras: banana republic. In the early twentieth century, they shipped so many bananas to America that banana peels became a public health threat. It's actually in the 1911 Boy Scout Manual – a scout's top two duties were: "Help an old lady across the street; remove a banana skin from the pavement so that people may not fall."

See that? There's two comedy clichés I mentioned at the top of the chapter. This shit has structure!

Honduras' banana business took a huge hit in 1998, when Hurricane Mitch drowned many of the crops. It's considered the worst hurricane of the past two hundred years, and the worst Mitch outside the US Senate. Hurricane Mitch destroyed as much as eighty percent of the banana crop. Many who worked in the banana business moved grudgingly into the hospitality business. And you should never, ever go into hospitality grudgingly. Just imagine you woke up tomorrow, and your home had turned overnight into a motel, and you had to serve breakfast to ME. You'd be pissed. Well, they're pissed, too.

They're especially bitter towards Costa Rica, a nearby country that went into the tourist business and actually made a go of it. Any time my driver in Honduras saw a driver go too fast, or too slow, too erratic or too cautious, he grumbled, "He drives like a Costa Rican." Still, that's one of those great discoveries you make when traveling: Every country has another country they hate. Malaysians complain about Banglasdeshis coming in to steal their jobs. Ecuadoreans don't like Venezuelans. And Libyans resent people who sneak in from Cameroon seeking a better way of life. Yes, Libya, where the living is easy.

Still, Honduras has a great ability to take a bad situation and make it much, much worse. When life gives them lemons, they throw the lemons at Costa Ricans. One day a teenage boy was our tour guide. He was excited that soon he'd be voting for President for the first time. "Who are you supporting?" I asked.

"The dictator."

"Wait, you know he's a dictator, but you're still voting for him?"

"I think he will be a good dictator."

Historical note: He wasn't. He was elected President and two days later, he fired the entire government. And since then, things have just gotten worse. When we visited the capital city of Tegucigalpa, it was famous for – well, nothing really. But now it has the second-highest homicide rate of any national capital. Watch your back, Caracas. Tegucigalpa is number two – with a bullet.

Another city we visited, San Pedro Sula, has been named the Most Dangerous Non-Warzone on Earth. It's also the birthplace of Carlos Mencia, who may be Honduras' greatest cultural export. If you haven't heard of him, 'Maxim' magazine called Mencia, "One of the worst comedians of all time." George Lopez said the comedian stole thirteen minutes of material from him; I couldn't believe it – George Lopez has thirteen minutes of material? Mencia is also accused of stealing jokes from Bill Cosby. Who do you root for in that story?

That's why I was so happy to be leaving Honduras. The tour company hired a car to take us to our next stop: Guatemala. The driver was a big angry man who looked and muttered like Bluto in the old Popeye cartoons. The trip got off to a bad start when he told us he needed to use an ATM. It was a hundred degrees out, and he left us standing on the hot asphalt of a mall parking lot for two hours. In a panic, my wife called the tour company. Moments later, the angry driver burst out of the mall, carrying a steak dinner to go for himself.

"Why you call my boss?" he thundered.

"We didn't know what happened to you!" my wife said.

He said, "I just go in to use the ATM! That is all!"

"I guess it's one of those ATM's that dispenses steak dinners," I said.

Now that we were all sweaty and angry, we set off on an eight-hour drive through the jungle. Minutes into the trip, the driver demanded, "Give me a hundred dollars or I will turn you out into the jungle."

"No," I replied.

"All right, one hundred quetzals." That's the local currency. He had immediately lowered his ransom demand to twelve dollars. He wasn't even a good kidnapper.

Again, I told him "no." I wasn't being heroic – I just wasn't paying attention. When he said he wanted a hundred dollars I thought he wanted to go to another ATM.

Now angrier than ever, he roared down the road, running over a rooster along the way.

"You just ran over a chicken," I said.

"I DON'T CARE!" Whoa, big man.

He drove us straight to Guatemala, doing ninety the whole way. We had prepaid him for lunch but he refused to stop for it. Yes, I was sixty years old and a bully stole my lunch money.

My week in Honduras was like a horror movie, right up to the shock ending. As we happily signed into our Guatemalan hotel, the monster returned! Our angry driver burst into the lobby waving a piece of paper.

"You have to sign this! Tell the company I did a good job."

We refused. He started yelling. The hotel clerk called the police, who dragged our driver away. Then, the Guatemalan clerk did something I hadn't seen all week in Honduras. He smiled. We had a great stay in Guatemala. The people were nice, the coffee was delicious, and the Mayan ruins are the best in the world. They are so haunting and otherworldly, a scene from the first "Star Wars" was shot there. The Millennium Falcon lands atop a Mayan ruin called Temple IV. Even Han Solo knew to skip Honduras.

It's a comforting rule of travel that every inhospitable country has a much nicer version of itself just across the border. Honduras has Guatemala. North Korea has South Korea. The US has Canada.

SIDE TRIP: The Case of the Gratuitous Gratuities

My wife and I checked into a hotel room in Mumbai, after traveling for what seemed like three days and passing through forty or fifty time zones. It was only eight at night, but I was ready to sleep. That's when Denise noticed a sign on the nightstand: "Free Fruit Plate – Dial 0 to Order – Available for a Short Time Only." I knew this was a lie, since the sign was varnished into the table – it was literally part of the furniture. I saw Denise reach for the phone. "Don't order it," I said. "Don't order it don't order it don't order it."

She ordered it.

We sat up for the next two hours, nervously anticipating the arrival of our magically free fruit plate. It never came. We finally collapsed from exhaustion.

An hour later, we were awakened by a knock. I groggily opened the door and saw a hotel employee standing there. Empty-handed. "Hi-eee," he chirped. "I was wondering if there's anything I can get you."

"Our fruit plate," I moaned. "We've been waiting three hours for our fruit plate."

"Oh, I am so sorry." He didn't move. He just hung in the doorway like Spanish moss. He wanted a tip, so I gave him five dollars – for what? I don't know. To thank him for waking me from a dead sleep and not bringing my fruit plate. He stared at the five like I had spit in his hand. I gave him another five and sent him on his way.

Denise and I sat up for another hour waiting for an order that never came. If you change "fruit plate" to "Godot," you'd have a Samuel Beckett play.

It finally arrived at one a.m. – three small slices of apple that had gone brown with advanced age, all sitting on a chipped saucer. The young man clung to the doorway like housepaint, awaiting a tip for this fruity abomination. I gave him ten dollars.

Two hours later, we were awakened a third time by a knock at the door. It was him again. "The kitchen needs the plate back," he explained. This was a five-hundred-room hotel in Mumbai, but apparently they were one chipped dish away from catastrophe. I gave him the plate and a ten-dollar tip for his heroic service.

The Japanese have a saying: "Free is the most expensive." In this case, a free fruit plate cost me thirty dollars and a good night's sleep. It's a tale where avarice meets aggravation in a location better known as…"The Tipping Point."

The weirdest part of this picture is that there are still pay phones.

Chapter 10

THE ULTIMATE TRIPS

I Get High: Kilimanjaro

Along, long time ago, my wife and I were watching TV, when a news bulletin came on: Sixty tourists had just been gunned down by terrorists outside of Cairo, Egypt. Denise turned to me and said, "We've gotta go!"

I asked, "Why?"

She said, "Because it won't be crowded!"

She was right about that, of course. I could think of sixty hotel rooms that just opened up.

READER: BOO!

Stop booing. The book's almost over.

A, short, short time ago, my wife and I were watching the Reese Witherspoon film "Wild." It's based on the brilliant best-seller by Cheryl Strayed I never read, nor intend to.

The film opens with Reese, halfway through a thousand-mile hike, tearing off her boots in disgust. Her feet are blistered and bloody. She hurls the boots into a ravine, uttering a pretty serious blasphemy. Then she yanks out her last remaining toenail with an agonized scream.

My wife turned to me. "We should take a hike like that!"

And so Denise booked us a flight to Tanzania, for a six-day hike up (and presumably down) Mt. Kilimanjaro. At nineteen thousand three hundred and thirty feet, Kilimanjaro is Africa's tallest peak. This would be a challenging hike for even a vigorous young athlete. And I am none of those things. I am a tubby middle-aged man from Manhattan. My weekly workout is an hour on the elliptical trainer (cumulative). Incline: 0. Reistance: 0. Doctors say this provides the same cardio benefits as a hot dog and a milkshake.

Most people train for a year to climb Kilimanjaro. We just got off a plane and started doing it. We hadn't even slept for twenty-four hours, thanks to a missed flight connection in Amsterdam.

The first leg of our six-day hike went straight up – it's a giant stairway cut into the foothills of the mountain. It's the equivalent of climbing two Empire State Buildings, or one of those crazy skyscrapers the Chinese are throwing up these days. At the start of the climb, I am in a tropical rainforest; soon it becomes a scrubby Alpine desert; by the end of the first day, I'll be in a moonscape, devoid of trees, plants, and animals. I will be spending Christmas week in a land where even moss is too smart to grow.

That, by the way, is the only description of scenery you're going to get in this story. When you hike up a mountain, you spend the entire time staring at your feet. Every step can maim or kill you. There are pebbles you can slip on, boulders that can crack your kneecap, potholes where you can twist an ankle, and gullies which can swallow you whole. Every pace is a calculation. Every step is like doing your taxes. This is what makes hiking so unbelievably dull.

I realize this early on, after what felt like two hours of climbing. I know it hasn't really been two hours – nothing dilates time quite like the boredom of hiking. It's probably been ninety minutes. Maybe just an hour. I look at my watch.

It's been eighteen minutes.

I'm not making that up. Hiking is so mind-numbingly dull, it exceeds all comic exaggeration. There's a scene like this in the movie "Interstellar." Matthew McConaughey leaves his spaceship and travels to the planet of CGI tidal waves. He's only gone for three hours, but due to wormholes or gravity or something, for his fellow astronauts it seemed like twenty-three years.

Three hours that can feel like twenty-three years. Hiking is like that. So is watching the movie "Interstellar."

Knowing this would happen, I brought along an iPod loaded with music to get me through the trip. That very first day, the iPod slipped out of my ears and fell down into the outhouse I was using. Was I going to dive into an African latrine to rescue a bunch of Smashmouth songs? I considered it.

I finish the first day's hike just as the sun is setting. I'm drained, cramped, and miserable. And yet, I've done it.

I've reached the very top of the very bottom of Kilimanjaro.

STARTING POINT
MACHAME ROUTE
WISHING YOU A GOOD CLIMB

Your first day's climb up Kilimanjaro starts like this... and ends like this.

DAY 2

We spent the night in a leaky, cold tent, then downed a bunch of breakfast biscuits with the amazing name "Tiffany's Glucose." Sleepy and undernourished, we began our second day's climb. And that's when I learned that the tour company had eight porters carrying our stuff. Did it really require eight strong men to keep me in abject squalor?

I began to think there was some padding in the payroll. Especially when I saw Wonderboy. This was a young African porter whose entire burden was twelve loaves of Wonder Bread dangling from his belt. It was an absurd sight. He resembled a scalphunter who'd raided a Midwestern Kroger's.

Twelve loaves of white bread! For two people for six days! Someone – probably the Synthetic Bread Council – convinced them that every American eats an entire loaf of Wonder Bread every day. And it wasn't even real Wonder Bread – it was a knock-off brand. It was Bemusement Bread.

It was fake fake bread.

My wife wouldn't touch the stuff. I ate a pity slice a day. I watched those loaves squooshing together as Wonder Boy walked, and thought: Ditch the bread. Carry me.

Our tour guide was a man named Anton. Although my wife heard it as "Irving," as if we'd found the one black Jewish guide in Tanzania. Denise had trouble with Anton/Irving's accent, causing her to hear some truly remarkable things. Like when he told us he goes to church "dressed as Santy Claus." (I think he said, "dressed in Sunday clothes." Either way, it's not something an Irving would say.)

Then she heard his candid confession that he couldn't be a fisherman, "because I am sissy." (I'm pretty sure he said "seasick.")

And when he said they greeted the Pope's visit by "waving flags" she thought the people were waving pigs. I wish I could see the things my wife hears.

At times during the hike I'd stop to look back at how far I'd come. All I could see was fog. Amorphous gray fog. Fog permanently sits around the base of Kilimanjaro. Unlike me, it knows better than to climb it.

Fog is not scenery – it's not even nothing. It's less than nothing. Even when you close your eyes you see something: white dots of light and multicolored threads floating around. Those threads are dead nerve cells swimming in your eyeball goo. (See, you learned something from this story! You'll learn one more fact on Day 5, so keep reading!)

When we reached our second night's campsite, I had to sign in at a park register. It's a massive old-

For most of the climb, fog is your scenery.

fashioned ledger, the kind Bob Cratchit was always scratching away at. They ask for a tremendous amount of information: name, signature, occupation, gender, passport number, permit number, tour group, tour leader. There's also a fair amount of redundancy – they ask for your nationality, country of origin, country issuing your passport, and citizenship. Once the register is full, it is tossed, unread, on a pile of other registers. There it will slowly crumble into dust.

The one other thing they ask for is age. I enter mine: At the time, I was fifty-five. Then I look at the other ages listed above me: nineteen, twenty-two, seventeen, twenty-four. I turn back page after page in the ledger, and the numbers are the same: twenty-four, twenty-seven, sixteen, nineteen, twenty-three, twenty-nine, eighteen, twenty-two, eighteen... Finally I spot one old geezer of thirty-three. That's when it hits me: I am the Old Man of the Mountain.

I'm not just the oldest man on Kilimanjaro – I could be the father of the next oldest man on Kilimanjaro. For the first time in my life I know I'm doing something I'm too old for.

Twenty-year-olds shouldn't go to high school proms.

Forty-year-olds shouldn't attend Burning Man.

And I shouldn't be climbing this fucking mountain.

DAY 3

The first two days' hiking were not bad: the first was a giant stairway, the second, a gradual, rolling ascent. This is all schmuck-bait. On the third day, once you've reached the point of no return, the path devolves to a nightmarish series of crags and ravines right out of "Lord of the Rings." I begin to see hiking as a metaphor for life: Every day is worse than the one before.

I tell my wife, "If you're not enjoying this, we can stop any time. I won't mind." It's the same trick I use when I take her to a horror movie and I'm scared out of my mind. It never works there either.

I do have one cute story. As we emerge from our tent one morning, Anton says, "I'll bet this is not as comfortable as your hut in New York."

So sweet. He thinks we live in a hut.

"I'll bet your hut has a radiator!"

I don't have the heart to tell him our hut in New York isn't much bigger than this tent. And it cost $1.5 million. Plus fifteen hundred a month in hut maintenance fees.

That's it. Six days hiking, one cute story.

Then Anton got down to business. "In two days we'll be climbing to the summit. Did you bring torches?"

I assumed he meant flashlights, and not those burning sticks you use to drive Frankenstein from your town. Whichever he meant, I didn't have them.

"Rain poncho? Rubber boots? Scarf? Thermal mittens? Thermal blanket?"

No, no, no, no, and no.

Anton regarded me like a man who brought a snorkel to a moon landing. "Did you at least bring rain pants?"

Rain pants? I know what snow pants are, but what the hell are rain pants? I do have pants that protect me from the rain. They're called pants.

Anton roared at me, "You need two pairs of rain pants!"

Whatever rain pants do, they must not do it very well. Otherwise you wouldn't need two pairs.

Anton gave me a look of deep disapproval, which masked an even deeper sense of disapproval. My father gave me this look once: It started when I was thirteen, and ended with his death in 2004. Perhaps Anton was Jewish after all.

As we climbed, Anton coached us: "Slowly, slowly." Twenty-two years as a guide, two hundred ascents of Kilimanjaro, and this was the only advice he could offer: "Slowly, slowly." Occasionally, he'd say it in Swahili: "Poley, poley."

I had expected to go bounding up the mountain like some Hemingway hero. Instead, I was forced to shuffle up it like a Tim Conway character. (For you youngsters, Tim Conway was a brilliant comic actor who used to play an old man. Then he was an old man. Now, he's not even that.)

The only other Swahili I learned was the word for hello: "yambo." Except sometimes they said "mambo." And occasionally "jambo." It seems like a small distinction, but it's the difference between greeting someone with "hello," "mellow," or "Jell-O." Mostly I just waved and tipped people.

As I slogged through that third day, I remembered an old news story: Three American hikers in Iraq had been arrested and thrown into an Iranian prison. Lucky them! They got to stop hiking and ate Persian food for four years.

Then I think back to "Wild," the movie that inspired this trip. But I can only remember one scene. It's a flashback, where Reese Witherspoon is working as a waitress, and she has sex with two customers in an alley behind the restaurant. I know this is supposed to depict her character's descent into numbed despair, but two thoughts rush immediately to mind:

- Man, that's hot.
- What do you tip a waitress for that?

That night, my wife and I lay side by side in our sleeping bags. We were jammed in a tent about the size of a deep freeze, but much colder. We both wore every stitch of clothing we'd brought – seven layers – and still we were freezing. Every part of us was chapped.

My wife stank. I stunk.

"If this were a U.N. refugee camp," I said, "Bono would visit and break into tears."

My wife laughed. "Maybe Sting will write a song about us."

"Maybe Angelina Jolie will adopt us," I replied.

It was nice. If we could laugh through this, the Apocalypse is going to be a snap.

Or maybe it was just oxygen deprivation.

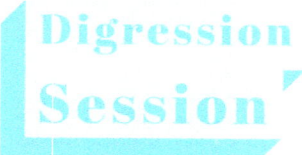

A Brief Digression on Danger

There are lots of things in travel that seem dangerous, but really aren't. Take whitewater rafting. If this were really dangerous, would they do it on corporate retreats?

I realized how non-threatening this was when we went rafting on the Nile. The water was at full churn when the tour guide said, "Jump out."

I said, "What?"

He said, "Jump out."

So I did. I was wearing a life vest, and I bounced around in the roiling waters like a cork. It was fun. You gotta really work hard to kill yourself whitewater rafting. Each year, two and a half million people try it, and less than ten die. If you crunch the numbers, that means you could whitewater raft every day for a hundred years before you died. And what are you doing rafting when you're a hundred years old? Lie down, grampa. Take a nap.

An even safer activity is ziplining. These places are popping up everywhere, because to build a zipline, all you need is a length of steel cable, and one point higher than another one: a mountain and a tree, a tree and a rock, a tall guy and a short guy. A basic zipline package includes four rides. The first time you go, it's scary; the second time, it's exciting; the third time, it's no big deal; the fourth time, your mind wanders; you find yourself thinking, "What does a postage stamp cost these days?"

But climbing a mountain is genuinely dangerous. We visited Zermatt, Switzerland, home of the Matterhorn. It's an amazing sight – God created an exact replica of the Matterhorn at Disneyland. Nonetheless, it's killed six hundred people – the mountain, not Disneyland. Zermatt has a special cemetery just for people who died on the Matterhorn. And it's not even that big a mountain. We were climbing one four thousand feet higher. It was Day Four of our hike up Kilimanjaro, and all Hell broke loose.

Day 4

Our guide has us climbing a sheer rock face of cracked boulders. There's no discernible trail – he's just scrambling and zigzagging around like a salamander. I begin to think he's improvising. No tourist has ever made it this far, and Anton is forced to ad lib.

All around us, our nimble porters are stumbling and falling. There's panic in our guide's eyes. The porter carrying a dozen loaves of Wonder Bread takes a terrific spill – he would have fractured his pelvis were it not cushioned by rubbery white bread.

This is all the result of altitude sickness: The air has gotten too thin.

Over the past four days, I've had to give up TV, cell phone, internet, coffee, hot showers, cold showers, electric lights, electric anything, clean clothes, sex, and toilets. Now, they've taken away my oxygen. I need that, man!

I also haven't seen a mirror in four days. This is probably a good thing. My beautiful wife now looks like a character from "The Grapes of Wrath." I started the trip ugly. By now I'm a Goya etching.

Amazingly, I'm the only one who is not suffering from the altitude. I believe this is because I'm a descendant of Moses. At the age of one hundred and fifty, Moses climbed Mt. Sinai (altitude: seven thousand four hundred and ninety-seven feet), where God handed him two heavy stone tablets. Moses schlepped them all the way down, only to smash them in anger at the bottom. So I'm not the first Jew to make a pointless climb up a mountain.

It's my non-Jewish wife who is suffering mightily. She's belching and puking from the altitude. At one point she collapses, landing face down on a rock, mouth open. She cracks her three front teeth.

I feel awful for her, of course. But… this trip was her idea – I wanted to go to Disneyworld.

Misery loves company, but it absolutely adores agony.

Misery can be a real dick.

And then, seventeen thousand feet up, with people collapsing all around me, I hear, "Are you Mike Reiss?"

I presumed it was the Angel of Death. It was actually a stand-up comedian from Brooklyn. He was a huge "Simpsons" fan, and he recognized me, something that happens approximately never. The man had me cornered on the side of a mountain in Africa. There was no escape. And so, for the next three hours, I used the last of my oxygen answering questions like, "Where is Springfield?" and "Why did you kill Maude Flanders?"

That night, I settled into bed in a tent the size of a fat man's coffin. Tomorrow I would climb to the summit of Mt. Kilimanjaro. I knew if I got a good night's rest – eight hours, ten hours – I could do it.

Two hours later, Anton rapped on my tent flap. "It's time to go," he said.

DAY 5

The final hike to the peak of Kilimanjaro begins at one a.m. I'm sure this was on some travel document I never got, listed right after "bring rain pants."

The most glorious scenery, the moment this whole week has been building to, and you are expected to do it in bitter cold and pitch darkness. My guess is that it started with a typo: the Tanzanian Tourist Board meant to say "one p.m.," but wrote "one a.m." by accident, and they've been doing it that way ever since.

More likely, some doofus decided it would be supercool to reach the summit at sunrise. Because it's not enough to climb Africa's highest peak, to look down into its yawning volcanic crater, to marvel at the snows that inspired a Hemingway novel. No, you need a sunrise, too.

Mind you, a sunrise is about the dullest thing the sun does. A solar eclipse is awesome. And a sunset has the decency to come at a pleasant hour. A sunset is also prettier than a sunrise, since the light is refracted through the dust that's been stirred up during the day. (Remember, on Day 2 I said you'd learn one fact Day 5? That was it. Sunsets are prettier than sunrises.)

We scramble up over another quarter mile of boulders. Today is just like yesterday, except we're doing it in the dark.

And suddenly, the boulders come to an end, giving way to a wide, gently sloping path. I can handle this. I'm going to saunter up to the peak of the mountain. I'm happy.

Just then, the path takes a sharp turn – straight up. The last leg of the trip is less a path than a wall. It's a path you can hang art on.

I'm Charlie Brown and the football. And Kilimanjaro is my Lucy.

I scramble and scratch my way up the trail. This is the worst day of my life, beating out the previous record-holder: yesterday. I'm depleted, I'm bored, I'm pissed at the mountain.

"How are you coming?" Anton asked.

"Slowly slowly," I said. I use the Swahili word. "Poley poley."

"You're too poley poley!" he snapped. I struggle onward and upward until finally I can see the top – I can even make out other hikers at the peak.

"How long till I get there?" I ask Anton. We'd already been hiking for five hours.

Anton replied, "In forty-five minutes, you'll be halfway there."

And that's when I said it. "I quit."

After five and a half days of solid hiking. A hundred yards vertically from the top. Ninety eight point three percent of the way up Kilimanjaro, I quit.

My wife elected to go on with the hike, demonstrating the same foolhardy persistence that has kept her in this marriage for thirty-four years. She continued on up with Anton. I went down alone. On the descent, I met three other quitters. It turns out people had been quitting the hike throughout the week. Many bailed after the first day. My vacation had an attrition rate like the Navy Seals Program.

I scampered down the mountain like a gazelle, eager to get back to my tent. I took just one break, stretching out on a large flat rock. I looked up at the most beautiful night sky I'd ever seen. Every constellation I'd ever heard of was up there shining brightly. The Milky Way glowed like a Broadway marquee.

I'd missed this all week. I'd been too busy looking at my feet.

I reached my tent around dawn and immediately conked out. I was awakened six hours later, as four porters carried my wife into the tent. She looked like a pile of laundry that had been roughed up by the Mob. But she'd made it to the peak.

"So hard… so hard…" she croaked. "Sensational… But so hard."

We'd taken completely different paths, but arrived at amazingly similar conclusions.

"Quitting that hike was the smartest thing I ever did," I said. "Next to marrying you."

"Climbing that mountain was the toughest thing I ever did," she said. "Next to getting you to marry me."

Then we both fell asleep.

DAY 6

It takes fifty hours – five ten-hour days, a Japanese workweek – to reach the peak of Mt. Kilimanjaro. It takes just five hours to climb all the way down. I know down is faster than up, but ten times as fast? Had we been climbing some Escher-like trail, always ascending but never getting higher? After I'd paid Anton and all those porters, he made a confession: "The longer we keep you on the mountain, the more money we make."

The descent was my favorite part of the trip, not just because gravity was on my side and I was getting off the damn mountain. It was an inspiring journey, as the lifeless rocks and boulders gave way to a lush tropical rainforest. Colobus monkeys swung through the jungle. They seemed to be chattering, "This is what you visit Africa to see, dumbass."

I knew my journey had ended when I saw something at the ranger station I hadn't seen in six days: a toilet. A filthy, seatless, smelly, broken toilet. I could have kissed it.

Could I have made it to the top? I was tired that night, but I probably had the energy. I just couldn't face another five hours of mind-boggling, brain-numbing, mom-calls-to-complain-about-her-knee boredom. Perhaps if I'd had some incentive. Maybe if there were a cash prize on top. Or if it somehow would convince Daniel Day-Lewis to make more films, or Nicolas Cage to make less.

But climbing it just to climb it wasn't enough. I didn't need to be the schmuck at a party telling people I conquered Kilimanjaro. My friends would say, "Hey, that's great," and think, "If Tubby did it, it can't be that hard."

The movie "Wild" ends with Reese Witherspoon finishing her hike at the Canadian border and having a bunch of epiphanies: life goes on. Time heals all wounds. Taking heroin is bad.

I'm not sure why she needed a thousand-mile hike to teach her this. My epiphany is that her epiphanies are bullshit. Some people will say anything to avoid going into Canada. But did I learn anything from all this? Was it like high school, where I learned a bunch of stuff I never use, like calculus and Latin? Or was it like college, where I learned nothing and actually forgot calculus and Latin. Yes, I came out of Harvard dumber than I went in.

But I did learn something from Kilimanjaro – sometimes it's okay to quit. As Americans we're taught, "You can do it. Never say die. Nothing is impossible." I'm telling you, "You can't do it. Say die. Some things are impossible." We couldn't win the Vietnam War and we couldn't learn the metric system. Stuff happens. Cut your losses, throw in the towel, try something else. This is why I'm no longer asked to give commencement addresses.

One thing I'm not giving up on is mountain climbing. On our next vacation, we plan to conquer the tallest mountains in Florida: Space Mountain, Big Thunder Mountain, and a Matterhorn that won't kill you. I'm going to Disneyworld!

I'll bet we can do it all in a day—it's a small world, after all. But I may stretch it out to a week. Poley poley.

I Get Low: The Titanic

If you haven't realized it yet – and the book is nearly over people! - my wife and I like danger. And by "my wife and I," I mean just my wife, not me, not even a little. People know this about us, so my friend Jay called with an invitation: "You guys wanna come to a party tonight? There's a good chance you will be killed."

This was not some cute murder mystery dinner party – this was the real thing. They were having a cocktail reception for Vladimir Putin's number one enemy. He was a marked man. We were excited until Jay added, "While you're at the party, I advise you not to eat or drink anything." This might have been a deal-breaker: I don't mind get shot or blown up, but I go to a party to eat.

We survived the evening. While the food wasn't poisoned, it was pretty bad – fried codfish balls. And the wine was from England. Yucch.

Another "friend" in Seattle told us about his neighbor who took passengers on deep dives in his homemade submarines. "This sounds like a good way to get killed," I said, and for once, I'm afraid I was right. In June 2023, his sub the Titan imploded on a dive to the Titanic. All five passengers died, including the sub's inventor, owner, and pilot, Stockton Rush.

They say name is destiny. Martin Short really is short. Fats Domino was pretty fat. And Cedric the Entertainer… looks like a Cedric. So when your name is Stockton Rush, you are fated to a life of adventure. Mr. Rush was as handsome and suave as a soap opera doctor. He'd had every career an eight-year-old boy could dream of: airline pilot, rocket scientist, inventor, and now submarine captain.

Our voyages with Captain Rush started small and grew, well, titanic. Our first trip left from an exotic port off a mysterious island known as… Staten. A hundred miles off Staten Island is Hudson Canyon, an underwater chasm the size of the Grand Canyon. We were going to dive it, in Rush's homemade sub. It was gleaming white and streamlined, like a "Star Wars" Tie Fighter or a high-end vape pen. The viewport was a giant acrylic eyeball, surrounded by spotlights and lasers. A towboat pulled the submarine, bobbing and bouncing as we headed out to sea.

The most dangerous part of riding this sub, the bit no one put a lot of thought into, was getting in the damn thing. They simply leaned a six-foot kitchen ladder against the floating submarine. You had to scramble up the ladder as it bobbed with the waves, leap over to a tiny entry hatch on top, then plunge blindly into the sub, dropping six feet into darkness.

Once you were in, it was groovy: cool, dimly lit, quiet. The sub's interior was about the same as a mini-van; it would seat five, if there were seats. Instead, five of us spread out on the carpeted floor: pilot, co-pilot, my wife, myself, and one other rich stupid tourist with a death wish. We sank noiselessly, peacefully to the bottom of the sea. One thousand feet down, the ocean floor looked like the landscape from a Road Runner cartoon: miles of sand, oddly shaped rocks, and the occasional coral branching out like a saguaro cactus. It was amazing.

It was only after we returned that Captain Rush told us we were the first people ever to go down there! I was the Neil Armstrong of Hudson Canyon. This would be great, except I don't want to be the Neil Armstrong of anything! I want to be the Harrison Schmitt – the twelfth and final man on the moon. He didn't go up till they got all the kinks out.

But Stockton Rush was emboldened by this success, and he wanted to go somewhere deeper. Thirteen times deeper. He wanted to take a sub to the Titanic, two and a half miles down. And my wife wanted us to go with him.

Two years later, Denise and I were standing on a dock in Newfoundland. Out in the harbor was the ship that would take us to the very spot where the Titanic sank. A rubber speedboat pulled up to take us to the ship, when the skipper realized, "Oh man, I forgot the life jackets!" This of course, was the same mistake the Titanic made.

Here we were: prosperous tourists risking our lives on an untested vehicle to see where other prosperous tourists lost their lives on an untested vehicle. Whatever. This was my wife's dream and my birthday gift to her. I had no idea what the trip cost and Denise wouldn't tell me. She told all our friends though, who would look at me and go, "You are some good husband," or "Wow! What a sap!" Both were correct.

Captain Rush built an all-new sub for this dive: The Titan! It sat on the deck of the ship, white and bulbous like an Imperial Storm Trooper's helmet from, again, "Star Wars." The porthole had to be much smaller – it was the size and shape of a window on a washing machine. In fact, that's where it may have come from.

The sub looked super-cool from the front. But in the back, it had a bunch of Styrofoam blocks randomly strapped on, to improve buoyancy. They said this was super high-tech styrofoam, but it looked like the stuff every '80s stereo came packed in. There were also two flotation tanks that looked like bulging eyes, and a landing pad that resembled a gaping mouth. The sub looked scared to death. So was I.

The launch of The Titan had many setbacks before getting to this point: There was the pandemic. There was bad weather and rough seas. Once, the sub got struck by lightning, frying the electronics. On a test dive, a system failure trapped everyone inside it for twenty-seven hours. And finally the submarine's toilet broke. This was troubling news, since the toilet was basically a potty seat – two pieces, no moving parts. They were explaining all these setbacks to us on a PowerPoint presentation when the computer died, too. Uh-oh.

Then they brought out waivers for us to sign. Here are some highlights:

- "While diving below the ocean surface I will be subject to extreme pressure and any failure of the vessel could cause severe injury or death."
- "I will be exposed to risks associated with high-pressure gases, pure oxygen, and high voltage systems which could lead to injury, disability, and death."
- "If I am injured I may not receive immediate medical attention."
- "Welcome aboard!"

We sailed for two days, three hundred miles into the North Atlantic. Many on the crew were Newfoundlanders, a people so insular they still had the Irish accent of their distant ancestors. They'd also never heard of "The Simpsons," the show I'd been working on for three decades. The one writing credit I had that excited them was "ALF," a series that was canceled thirty-five years ago. Here's a verbatim exchange:

SEA COOK (IRISH LILT): ALF was some character. Can I call you Alfie?

ME: I'd rather you didn't.

SEA COOK: Ah, you're a funny one, Uncle Alfie.

ME: So now I'm your uncle?

I emailed Paul Fusco, the creator of "ALF," to tell him there was a pocket of die-hard fans onboard this ship. He wrote back, "Next trip, sell merchandise."

The day finally arrived – we were anchored two miles above the wreck of the Titanic. They outfitted my wife and me in matching navy blue flight suits. It was supposed to make us feel like crew members, but I just felt like an idiot. It's like when you put a fire chief's helmet on a five-year-old. He may look cute, but he won't be putting out any fires.

We were now ready to board the submarine – we just had to take a Covid test. I passed mine. Denise failed hers. My wife, who had traveled to every continent since the pandemic began, had avoided catching Covid for two and a half years. But somehow she'd contracted it on this tiny boat in the North Atlantic.

Captain Rush said, "Sorry Denise, you can't take the trip. But Mike, you can still go!"

I said, "I don't wanna go!"

It's as if Neil Armstrong were getting ready to go to the moon when he came down with the flu. So NASA tells his wife, "You can go to the moon instead."

Yes, I'm comparing myself to Mrs. Neil Armstrong. But at Denise's insistence, I got on that sub and began a two-hour descent straight to the bottom of the sea.

The number of disasters preceding this trip was pretty amazing when you see how simple a mini-sub is. It's basically a car that you drunkenly drove into the ocean. It sinks like a stone until it finally hits bottom. When you want to come up, you drop some of your weights, and pop to the surface like a cork. That's it: Sink like a stone, pop up like a cork.

If they want to tilt the sub down, the pilot yells, "Everyone pile into the front. Hurry, hurry." To tilt it up: "Get in the back, move it, move it!"

To steer the sub, the pilot uses an Xbox game controller. I don't mean it looks like one – it's an actual joystick from a gaming system.

How can I describe my voyage to the bottom of the sea? It was… boring. The ocean here is pretty empty, so there was nothing to see out the porthole. I actually fell asleep. And if you want a shock, try waking up from a nap thinking you're home in bed, and realizing you're in a steel tube, two miles underwater, and sinking.

We touched bottom amid the usual assortment of catastrophes. We were nowhere near the Titanic. There were underwater currents pushing us farther and farther in the wrong direction. The sonar wasn't working and the compass kept flopping from east to west, north to south. There was also a time crunch. We had started late and there was a hurricane rolling in on the surface. Just another day in the life of Captain Stockton Rush.

A navigator on the surface was sending us directions but they did not conform to what we were seeing. The Russian science officer kept radioing the surface: "We need better directions. Switch to the B map."

The crew on the surface replied, "What is the B map?"

There were five of us in the sub, and four were working on the navigation. I was just one hundred eighty pounds of Jewish ballast.

The Russian kept up the pressure, radioing, "You must switch to the B map immediately!"

The crew responded, "There is no B map! We don't know what you're talking about!"

And finally, with just minutes before we had to give up, we saw it: the bow of the Titanic. We had twenty minutes to snap selfies with the famous parts, the bits you've seen in a million documentaries: the railing, the prow, the anchor. It wasn't overwhelming, it wasn't underwhelming. It was whelming.

Just prior to this trip, we'd been to Vegas, where every show has a VIP package: pay fifty bucks extra, and you get to go backstage afterwards. You shake hands with the star, you get your photo with them, you get the hell out of there. I'd wound up on the Titanic VIP package. This wasn't an adventure, it was a photo op.

The only real danger came in the last minute of the voyage. As the sub was being hoisted back onto the ship, the whole thing flipped vertical. Everything in the sub – computers, phones, five people and their sandwiches – crashed in a heap at the bottom of the sub. A trip to the Titanic ended in disaster.

Only when the voyage ended did I realize the import of what I'd done. Captain Rush told me, "More people have been in outer space than have done what you did yesterday." A passenger from Guadalajara became the first Mexican ever to reach the Titanic. As for me, I became the first "ALF" writer to get there. Take that, Mrs. Neil Armstrong!

The next day Captain Rush had another dive and it went perfectly. They had two solid hours to explore the wreckage, from stem to stern, from starboard to the other one. It was a glorious adventure and I missed it all. I'd stayed behind on the ship, ministering to my Covid-y wife. She was quarantined in her stateroom, sitting in the dark, demanding food: "Bring me fruit!"

I ran down two flights to the galley, loaded trays with watermelon, and ran them back up to her. But it was never enough. For a sick and slender woman, her appetite was ravenous: "MORE FRUIT!"

It was like serving a dragon. A vegan dragon.

Denise was already planning a return voyage, so we could visit the Titanic together. That trip I never wanted to take? I'd be taking it twice. Whatever it cost me, I'd be paying double.

But it was not to be.

Stockton Rush had an impossible vision, but he made it happen a dozen times. Finally, his luck ran out, as luck will always do. In June 2023, the Titan imploded. In a fraction of a second, Rush and his four passengers were killed, literally vaporized. The story galvanized the world, and the public demanded answers. But when someone dies climbing Mount Everest, it's not always the fault of the ropes or the tools or even the Sherpa who brought them there. Sometimes you just have to blame the mountain.

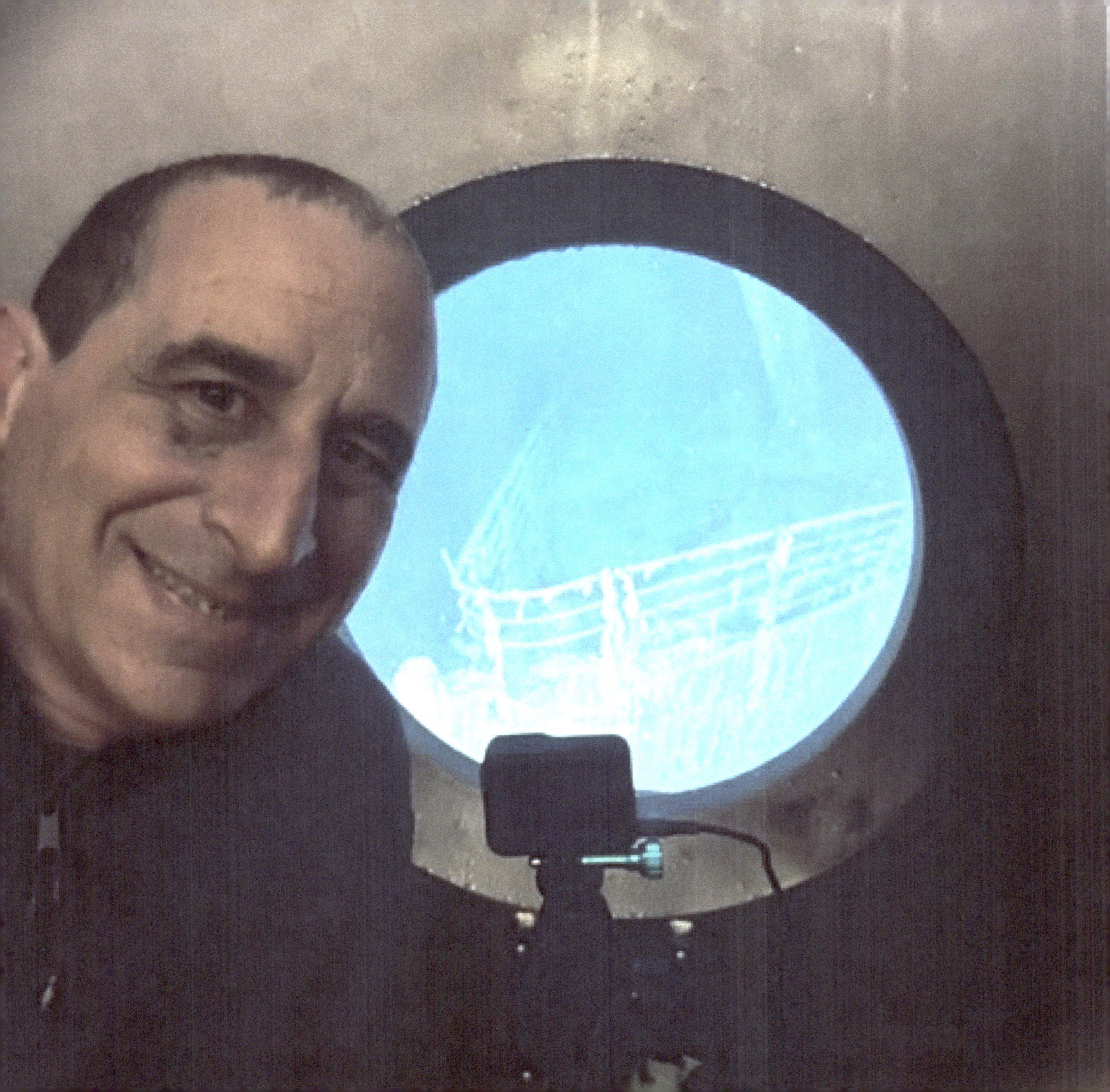

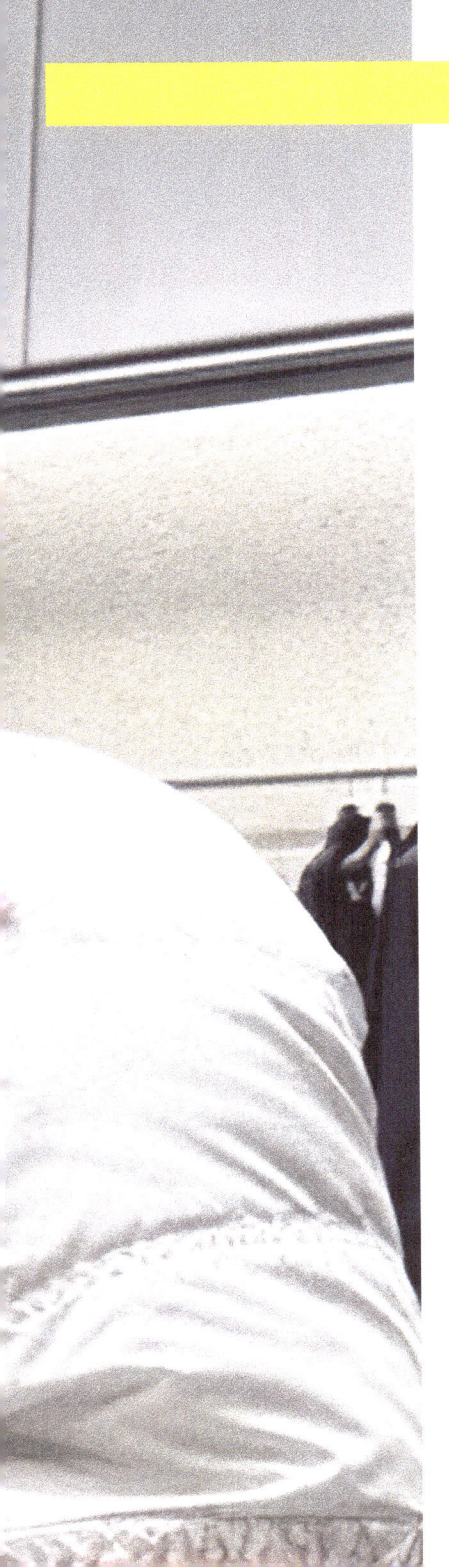

Chapter 11

NOW I'VE SEEN EVERYTHING

've visited one hundred thirty-four countries. I've walked on every continent and sailed on every sea. I took a sub to the ocean floor and nearly climbed Africa's tallest peak. None of it willingly. My wife dragged me to all these places and that's why I love her madly. If not for her, I'd have spent the past few decades, sitting on my fat ass watching YouTube. (I love "Pitch Meeting" and "guilty dog" videos.) Instead, I've seen amazing sights and eaten strange and wonderful food. But my favorite part was the people, meeting my fellow human beings. In every country I found people who were friendly, funny, and flattered someone would travel so far to see how they live. They were all like us… but different enough to keep life interesting. And I only got kidnapped once.

Now I've seen everything. Where else can my lovely wife drag me?

Mars!

Back in 2018, Earth was closer to Mars than it had been in centuries. Two civilian flights to Mars were planned to take advantage of this. One was a Dutch reality show that intended to send twenty-five passengers to colonize Mars. There was no plan to bring them back. They were sending them there to die. The show got two hundred fifty thousand applicants.

A more serious mission was planned to send two astronauts to circle Mars, take photos, and hopefully return. There was a one-in-three shot of dying from radiation sickness, and a ninety percent chance of getting cancer from the trip. The organizers were looking for a childless, middle-aged married couple on the premise that if they died, who cared?

Denise signed us up.

For her, it was the adventure of a lifetime. For me, it was a year and a half of free food and board. For once, I was in. I even had a selling point: I could write funny tweets from Mars. America's space program is a story of technological triumph and raw courage. But can you think of one funny thing any astronaut ever said? Sixty years without one good joke. Neil Armstrong: great American, lousy comic.

Surprisingly, Neil deGrasse Tyson endorsed us, saying, "If any couple could do this, it should be you." We knew him from college – of course, back then he was just known as Neil Tyson, possibly because he smoked deGrasse.

We took a trip to Purdue University to see a model of our spaceship. It was about the size of an RV. Most people couldn't imagine spending eighteen months in something this small. But we were New York apartment dwellers, used to cramped spaces. A place this big in Manhattan would go for three grand a month.

Believe it or not, we made it to the second tier of applicants before both Mars expeditions fell apart. The one we wanted to go on failed for lack of financing – an internet tycoon donated the first billion dollars, but no one would put up the other five. As for the Dutch reality show, they only had twenty-eight thousand dollars. That wouldn't get you to Mars by bus. If only the public knew the mission might kill me, they'd have chipped in. Ah well. That's one small loss for man, one giant loss for funny tweets.

Acknowledgments

Every writer wants do a travel book and no publisher wants to print one. An editor reviewed this manuscript and informed me, "I have, like, six thousand of these on my desk."

That's why I am so grateful to Marty Dundics for turning my travel stories into this gorgeous book. Marty, you've made my dreams come true and my travel deductible.

Much of this material first appeared in Michael Gerber's *American Bystander* magazine.

Even more of it appeared in my podcast "What Am I Doing Here?" Thanks to my great podcast producer Josh Perilo, and my one-man voice cast Trevor Morris, the funny doorman from my building. And thanks to the Bleav network for Bleaving in me

Xeth Feinberg, my collaborator for a quarter century, provided the wonderful cover and incidental art for this book.

Most importantly, thanks to my incandescent wife Denise. You dragged me into this life of constant adventure and snapped photos all along the way. Without you, this book would be six pages long.

About The Author

Mike Reiss has won four Emmys and two Peabody Awards during his thirty-five years writing for "The Simpsons". He ran the show in Season 4, which Entertainment Weekly called "the greatest season of the greatest show in history."

Reiss has been a contributing writer to more than two dozen animated films -- including four ICE AGEs, two DESPICABLE MEs, THE LORAX, RIO, KUNG FU PANDA 3, and THE SIMPSONS MOVIE – with a worldwide gross of $14 billion. He is an award-winning playwright and mystery writer, and an Emmy-nominated songwriter.

Mike has written twenty-one children's books, as well as "Springfield Confidential", a best-selling memoir of his three decades at The Simpsons. "Springfield Confidential" has been translated into German, Spanish, Russian and Czech, and was finalist for the Thurber Prize in American Humor.

Reiss hosts the podcast "What Am I Doing Here?" about his travels to 134 countries. He's climbed Mount Kilimanjaro, taken a submarine to the wreck of the Titanic, and been everywhere from the North Pole to North Korea.

Mike Reiss has written jokes for such comedy legends as Johnny Carson, Joan Rivers, Garry Shandling… and Pope Francis! For his comedic contributions to the charitable group Joke with the Pope, in 2015 Pope Francis declared Reiss "A Missionary of Joy".